Dedicated to Diego and Hunter Baron

Soul Driver

By

Peter B Baron

On the 22nd floor of a Manhattan high rise is a man. This is no ordinary man. This is a man that was raised as an orphan and was as poor as they come. When he was a little boy, before his parents were killed in a car accident, he lived in the poorest part of New Orleans. He used to walk two miles to school because there was no transportation and his parents had little money. Yet, despite all the things he didn't have, he was always happy and laughing. He remembers, like it was yesterday, what his mother used to say. "Life is great, as long as we have each other," is what seemed to come out of her mouth each and every day. She always had a way of making things seem okay.

Then came the day he was told that his parents died when someone ran them over as they were walking to the store. He was only 8 years old. If his parents hadn't have dropped him off to play with the neighbor's kid, he surely would have been killed too. It's a day that he tries desperately not to remember, but he can't. He has thought about it every day of his life ever since. Every night he replays the last hug and the last words he shared with his parents. He sure does miss them.

There were no other family members available to take care of him. The neighbors liked him but were unwilling to bring on another mouth to feed, so they watched him get put into a group home. The conditions at the home were terrible. It often felt more like a prison. The food was sparse and kids were always getting into fights and then punished. He hated that place and always dreamed of the day he would be able to leave. But, what bothered him most was watching people get picked on for no reason. The staff would ask few questions but hit a lot. Many times, they hit kids that didn't do anything.

Even though he knew he would suffer, he often spoke up for those that didn't speak up for themselves. Because of that, he was the most beat child at the home. He would stare out the window constantly looking at the fence they were told to never climb over. "The punishment will be severe if anyone ever tries to go over the fence," is what the staff would say. He knew they were not idle threats and the rest of the children were terrified to even go near it. It was tough being a young black man with nobody by his side.

One evening he heard noises on the other side of the fence. It was off in the distance and faint, but he heard what sounded like a woman asking for help. He knew that being outside that late would give the staff all the reason they need to get physical again. However, something inside of him drives him to help. He snuck out quietly without anyone noticing and made his way to the voice. He looked through the opening between the planks and noticed a woman on the ground. The woman looked like she had been there for a while and was in shock. "Are you alright?" he asked. The woman replied by saying "I have broken my leg and can't move. I was riding my horse when she bucked and tossed me off."

Realizing that the woman needed help right away, he looked around and asked "Where do you live?" She pointed to a house in the distance and said "Over there." He decided to climb over the fence and told the woman that he was going to run over to her house and try to get some help. He ran as fast as he could through the trees and brush and finally made it to the house. He just assumed that somebody would be around to lend a hand. However, after repeated attempts at knocking on the door, nobody answered. With few options, he broke the back window and climbed in. He frantically looked around for the phone to call for help. After he found it, he called the emergency number written on the phone and did his best to describe where she was. He ran back to her. As he sat with her, waiting for help, he was surprised to see police officers approach. He had just asked for an ambulance.

Immediately, the police ordered him away from the woman and tossed him in the back of the car. As the one officer tended to the woman, who had passed out, the other interrogated him and was convinced that he had something to do with it. "I'm not fooling around! What did you do to her?" the officer shouted in an abnormally angry way. "Nothing!" he replied. He kept repeating "I was just trying to help her," as the car door slammed shut.

4

Apparently, that officer knew the woman who was hurt and unresponsive. They went to the same church. When the ambulance finally arrived and took the young woman to the hospital, the police took Marcus to the police station. During the drive to the station, the same officer looked directly at him and said "For your sake, she better be alright." After a number of hours, he still sat in jail.

Meanwhile, back at the group home, staff members discovered that Marcus was missing. "Where is that trouble maker?" asked an old nasty woman as she looked at his empty bed. One of the boys, who thought he was going to fall into their good graces, told on him. "He went over the fence," he said. Marcus had helped defend that kid on a couple of occasions so it's almost fitting that instead of being praised for telling on Marcus, the boy was pulled into the other room and spanked for not telling them earlier.

In the hospital, the young woman came around while in bed. It happened to be that her friend, the officer, had come to check on her at the same time. She had just opened her eyes when he entered. She was happy to see him. "Are you alright Michelle?" he asked. Looking down at her leg, she said "Other than my leg killing me, I'll be fine. What are you doing here Bill?" The officer responded by telling her that they were called to the scene and found her unconscious near the fence. He was happy to add that they caught the guy that attacked her. "He had also broken into your house, so we got him for breaking and entering as well," he said.

The woman, who was in her mid 30's, was quick to correct him "No, No, he helped me. He saved me. He must have broken in to call for help," she said. Realizing his mistake, he called the station to let them know of the new information and have him released. At the station, Marcus had given the police the name of the group home where he lived. Upon receiving the updated information, the Police called the home to request that someone come pick him up. You would think they could have given the guy a ride back. As predicted, the staff was furious and despite his heroics, they were mad that he didn't obey orders in the first place. The beating was the worst one yet. Belt marks covered his back. He was still a kid and cried because of the pain but it eventually went away. The weeks passed as Michelle was at home recovering. Not for a minute did she suspect anything bad was going on at the facility on the other side of the fence. She just heard a number of kids in the distance and assumed everything was fine. Dressed in her cast and accompanied by crutches, she felt compelled to take herself to where the boy came from. She couldn't wait a minute longer to give him a big hug and thank him.

As she got out of her car and hobbled to the front door, she heard a man yell "Get back here and take it!" That was followed up by a boy screaming. She opens up the door and immediately asked in a loud voice "What the hell is going on around here?" A woman entered the front office and replied by saying "Can I help you?" in an irritated way. Michelle asked again "What's going on? Why is that boy screaming?" The no personality, sorry excuse for a caregiver, answered back with "It's just a kid acting up. He is always causing a problem. If you will excuse me, I need to get back to what I was doing." As the woman turned to exit the room, Michelle said "I'm here to see Marcus." The woman looked at her "There is no Marcus here," she said as she shut the door.

What that woman didn't realize is that you don't mess around with Michelle. She is a self made woman. Even at the young age of 37, she had managed to buy her own home and carve out a nice career in Marketing. Her parents were loving parents and had a little bit of money, but she managed to do it on her own, without the use of their money. Her folks spent a great deal of money raising her and putting her through college but after that, she took over. They taught her well and she was a good student.

Michelle didn't believe the woman and sensed something was wrong. Instead of going home she headed to the police station and talked with her officer friend. "I'm telling you Bill, something is not right there. They said that they had no Marcus and a kid was screaming like crazy. Please come with me tomorrow," she said. Even though he was not going to be able to do anything on the spot because they had no evidence, he said he would meet her there during his lunch break.

The next day, Bill met her there just as planned. As they both walked into the office, the woman at the front desk was caught off guard. She forgot to shut the door behind her when she noticed a uniformed officer next to the same woman she ran into. It's funny how this time she is all smiles. Before the woman even had a chance to say anything, Michelle looked through the opening of the door and actually saw Marcus sitting there in a chair as a man stood in front of him. "That is him right there!" she yelled while pointing to the other room. That lady was busted! "Bring him out here right now," said the officer.

When Marcus was brought out to the front and made eye contact with Michelle, he smiled. She limped over and gave him a big hug. While doing that, she felt him tense up. She let go, looked at him, and saw a grimace on his face. She pretended to give him another hug but that time she's didn't apply any pressure and whispered in his ear. "Is everything alright?" she asked. The young man was afraid to say anything for fear that once they left, he would get an even worse beating. He was a little scared then and you could see it in his face. The woman he helped was there with that officer who was so quick to blame him. However, she asked if he was alright and nobody had done that since his parents died.

Marcus took a chance. "They hit my back all the time for nothing," he whispered in her ear. Oh, she was pissed! Without asking, she lifted his shirt to expose his back. She was horrified and the officer was shocked when she turned him around to see his back. Fresh welts and new scars covered this gentle soul's back. She put his shirt down and said "You are coming with me!" The man who had come out from the back room said "He can't go anywhere. He stays here!" That is when the officer said "I don't think so! He is coming with us." He then bent down to look at the boy at his same level and said "I'm very sorry son. I should have believed you. Please forgive me." This amazing young man put his hand out to shake that of the officer's and said "It's alright."

They all headed back to the police station. Marcus gave complete details of who did what and how often. After a while, enough information was gathered to issue arrest warrants for each and every staff member at the facility. Michelle was also given temporary custody of Marcus.

He was thrilled at the idea of being out of there. The next day, officials and officers of all kinds appeared at the home and took the staff members away in handcuffs, much to the delight of all the children. You could see them through the windows cheering. A couple individuals from social services had been assigned to take over and run the place until other homes could be found for the kids.

One month later, all the kids were placed in other group homes and that one had been closed down permanently. During that month, Michelle nursed Marcus's wounds and worked the system to get full custody of him. It didn't matter to her that he is black and she is white. There will be people that talk and even look down on her, but they didn't save her, Marcus did. He deserves to be saved.

Over a couple of years, Marcus and Michelle became very close. The spare room in her house became his room. She was like a big sister to him and they did everything together. They went to church on Sundays, they ate dinner together and she taught him what it takes to do well in school. Marcus was a sharp young man and he too did well in school. He stayed at the house all through high school with very little drama from outsiders. On graduation day, Michelle proudly watched this wonderful young man accept his diploma. "The world is yours," is what he remembers her telling him.

Now, on this day, some 40 years later, he finds out she just died. They still spoke often after he moved out and went to college, but he had not talked to her in a little over a month. An attorney contacted him to let him know that she suddenly became seriously ill and died. He went on to tell Marcus how she left him some things in her will. The news comes as a shock to Marcus who was just in the middle of closing a big deal. He had retreated back into his beautiful office and just began staring out the window towards the street below. "All those people just trying to make it," he says out loud.

Even after all these years and all the struggles he still gives "Thanks" every night. He could have had the worst day ever and he still gives "Thanks." If he ever accidentally falls asleep without doing so, he feels guilty the next day and apologizes to the heavens. Even though he is a grown man, he still misses his parents on the same level that he did on the day he found out. He knows that it wasn't his fault but that hasn't stopped him from torturing himself mentally for not dying with them. Ever since then, he has looked at his life like work. He just wants to do as much as he can and go home to his parents.

The best part of life for Marcus is when he watches people get help when they so desperately need it. That's also why his wife left him. Even though she lived a nice lifestyle because Marcus makes good money, it never seemed to be enough for her and it would drive the woman crazy when he would spend some of the money that he made on other people. His office is beautiful because he has good taste and a sense of style, not because he spent a million dollars on it. He drives an average car but keeps it in good shape. He also enjoys the little things in life like watching a ball game on television or reading a good book. Marcus is a millionaire but you would never know it. When he got out of college he went into investment banking and is now a very successful portfolio manager. He liked the idea of securing people's financial future but the last few years he has felt a little empty doing it because most already had enough money to get through life in decent shape.

It's tough going through life when you care about the well being of others. So many people need help. So many people need a break. Many people can't be saved because they have given up, but it hurts him to see souls that have finished trying. He is only one man but he wishes he could be many. Marcus always wanted children but when he got married, his wife changed her mind and decided she didn't want any. That hurt him. Since then, he has not been able to make a connection with anyone on that level. Instead, he works.

So much is going through his mind as he stares out the window that he feels overwhelmed and tells his secretary that he is done for the day and that he will be back tomorrow. Marcus grabs his coat to deal with the cold that winters in New York bring. "Take the rest of the day off," he says to his secretary as he closes the door behind him. Two minutes later he returns and says "I almost forgot." The look on Cheryl's face is that of pure relief. She thought he changed his mind and wasn't going to give her that pay advance that she so desperately needs today. She and her family are 3 months late in paying the mortgage and her husband just got laid off. He is 57 years old and after 22 years with the same company he is now jobless.

The state of the economy is wreaking havoc on everyone. Even Marcus is struggling. Many of his customers have taken cash positions or have left the stock market entirely. It's not like it was a few years ago. He wishes he could hire her husband but there isn't enough for Cheryl to do. "That was five hundred you said?" he asks her. "Yes, thank you so much Marcus. I really appreciate it," she replies. He pulls out the check, hands it to her, and says "This is not an advance or a loan. This is to have. Plus, I am giving you a 20% raise. She looks down and notices that it is in the amount of $2,000.00. She starts to cry and gives him the biggest hug ever. "I wish I could do more but I can't at the moment," says Marcus. "God bless you Marcus," she says as he leaves again.

Leaving the lobby of the building, which he considers to be his second home, the winds howl. At the moment, there is no snow covering the ground but it's seriously cold. The forecast says to expect temperatures in the 20's for the rest of the week. Like most, Marcus has taken the subway into the city. As he boards the jam packed car, he looks into the faces of those standing near him. He can't understand why more people aren't smiling. There seems to be an unwritten rule, that if you are not a tourist, no smiling is allowed. Perhaps the other passengers will think you are weak and will look to pounce. He has never bought into that and usually seems to being the only one saying "Hi" to complete strangers.

After the thirty five minute ride on the subway, he begins his six block walk to his car. It seems to be as close as he can manage to get to the station. From there, it's only a twenty minute drive to his house. It's a modest house, but it's all paid for and in good shape. With his briefcase in hand, he pinches the top of his coat together to fight off the freezing wind. Above ground, a few blocks away, he comes across a woman in a wheelchair with nothing more than a sweater on top. They are moving in the same direction at the moment. She catches up to him and slowly begins to pass. "Wait a minute," says Marcus. "You are going to freeze to death like that," he adds.

The shivering woman stops for a moment and says "I'm just trying to make it back to the homeless shelter." As much as he would like to, he knows he can't save everyone from everything. However, he takes his coat off and hands it to her. "This should help," he says. Marcus forgets that he hasn't been feeling that well lately and catching pneumonia may kill him. He walks as fast as he possibly can until he gets to his car. It was just as far to get to his car as it was to walk back to the station and try to get a cab. He is freezing. He feverishly blows into his hands in an attempt to warm up before the heater in the car kicks in. He would have driven the woman but he remembers that the shelter is only a block away from where they were and she would get there quicker if she just carried on.

Finally, Marcus gets home and he has never been happier to be there. He heads straight to the kitchen to make a hot cup of coffee. Just as he sits down and takes his first sip, a knock on the door is heard. It's his elderly neighbor Mrs. Morgan.

She must be in her 80's and she's just the nicest person. She knows that Marcus lives by himself now so she brings him things like soup and fruit cakes. This time she asks if he can come over, as he does three or four times each winter, and fix her heater. It's very old and seems to always be giving her a hard time. "Of course my dear," he says as he grabs a couple of wrenches.

He can't believe how cold it is in there and says "You can't stay in here when it's like this." He seems more bothered than she is. After a few minutes and some turns of a wrench, the heater starts again. It generates the heat slowly and the woman has been dealing with it like this for years. She is old, with only one daughter, and lives off of the tiny social security checks she gets. Marcus has tried multiple times to get her to move into his place so he can try to take care of her but she won't give up her independence. "The moment I can't take care of myself is the moment I don't want to live anymore," is what she says.

The next morning Marcus calls his office and tells Cheryl that he won't be going in today. "I've got something that I need to take care of," he says. He then picks up the phone and calls a heating specialist. He knows he is going to pay a premium for a company to start work this afternoon, but he is alright with that. He is not one to waste money but time is of the essence in this case. Mrs. Morgan, as she prefers to be called, even though her husband died 25 years ago, deserves better. Marcus thought he would always be there to help Mrs. Morgan with the heater, but after hearing the news about Michelle today, he worries about his own well being. The suddenness of things has now got him worried about the nice little old lady next door. He doesn't want her to have to depend on him to keep warm. She should be comfortable all the time.

Both of their homes are the same size and designed the same way, so Marcus gives the square footage estimate to the owner of Mike's Heating & Air Conditioning. "How much did you say to install a new central air conditioning system?" he asks. Mike says "Eight thousand. There is a lot of work to do." Marcus can't believe how expensive it is but decides to do it and tells him to start immediately. Now for the fun part, he gets to go tell her. When Marcus returns to Mrs. Morgan's house, she is surprised to see him. It's rare that she has company.

Mrs. Morgan spends most of her day reading or baking and watches some television here and there. It never fails; she always has a whole fruit cake wrapped up and ready to go. "Wait right here," she says as she slowly turns around with her walker. Marcus says "No, it's alright. Thank you so much, but I didn't come for a fruit cake." She turns back around and says "Oh, you must have forgotten something then." That is when, with a big smile, Marcus says "I hope it will be alright with you. I took the liberty to invite some people over here today to install a whole new heating system." Mrs. Morgan is also a little hard of hearing so she says "What did you just say?"

Marcus puts his arm around her shoulder and speaks into her good ear. "I am having some men put in a new heating and air conditioning system that will work perfectly. They are coming today and they say it will take two days." The look that comes over her face is worth every penny. She is so happy. Then, when Marcus tells her not to worry about it because he is not only paying for the new system but he will be paying father was the best. Nothing in the world was more important than the well being of his beautiful son. Every child deserves a father like Marcus's father was.

As Marcus grabs another coat and heads out the door, it begins to snow. He is happy not to be going to the office and seems to have lost the desire to be there at all. He gets into his car and lets it warm up in the driveway while he grabs a piece of scratch paper from his glove box. He pulls a pen from his jacket and uses the steering wheel as a makeshift desk. He writes down a bunch of dollar amounts including the money spent on the heating system, his modified monthly expenditures, perceived value of his home, his total savings, and other things. It's not like it used to be but he feels that he doesn't need as much as what he thought he would need.

Marcus had always planned on having a wife and a couple of kids. He wanted to be able to provide a good life for them. After ten years of marriage and his wife continually waffling on having kids, the time seems to have passed. Marcus loved his wife and stuck in there until she thought it was the right time for her. It was always

her utility bills from now on, it's almost more than she can stand. She begins to cry and says "God bless you Marcus, you have a good soul," as she hugs him. She then adds "I better go make some more fruit cakes."

Two days later the system is up and running without a hitch. Coming back home from the office, Marcus stops next door to check on things and make sure she is alright. When Mrs. Morgan opens the door this time it's a perfect 72 degrees and it's the first time in ten winters that he has not seen her with a blanket of some kind wrapped around her shoulders. Everything is perfect and he's glad he was able to help her. She is still independent.

It was another tough day at the office. It has been that way for too long now. That deal he was working on the other day fell through because he didn't act in time. It was his first real chance he had to make some money in the last six months. On top of that, many of his clients have seen their portfolios hit very hard despite him moving them to so called "Safer positions." They call him, and for the first time ever, many of them begin to complain that it's his fault. They are used to making money, not losing a lot of it. He has actually lost three clients in the last two weeks. That has never happened before. The whole thing is making him very uneasy.

He is reflecting on things quite a lot as he sits in his kitchen watching the news. Despite being a very intelligent man, if he is looking to feel better about things, watching the news is not the thing to do. However, he watches anyway as he waits five more minutes for his TV dinner to finish cooking in the oven. The broadcaster begins to talk about a local homeless shelter that is going to have to shut its doors because of the lack of funding. "Donations have all but dried up these days," he says. Marcus can't believe his eyes when in the background he notices what looks like the same woman he saw the other day and she appears to still be wearing his coat. His eyes are glued to the set as he sees her sitting down on some portable bed with a young man that is studying.

A sick feeling comes over him as he thinks about that young boy in that situation. There is no way he can live his life like this when that poor boy has to live his life like that. He forgets his

dinner in the oven and falls asleep on the cou[ch] The next morning he calls Cheryl at the office says "I'm sorry. Something else has come up a I won't be able to make it in today. I will see y tomorrow." Cheryl says "No problem," but sh beginning to worry about him because he isn't acting normal. He still has a great big smile everyday and always sounds upbeat but he has never missed work before and all of a sudden is not showing up that much. As long as the o stays open and she shows up, she will continu get paid.

She suspects something is wrong with hi and she is right. He feels like he let Michelle d because he wasn't there. He had thanked her a million times for everything she had done for but she was the closest thing to family he had. feels alone all over again. Marcus is happy to b alive and is in no rush for things to end. If he could live life again and again he would. Howe with the way his life has gone, he feels like it's mainly a job. It's a job that he really enjoys. He also believes that his parents are watching and wants to make them proud of him. His father taught him at an early age to think of others. H going to be the right time for him. It came as a complete shock when she told him that she wanted out because of his constant desire to help others. Most people would have embraced such an idea but for some reason she always had to be the center of attention and when he spent any time thinking of the well being of others, it became a threat to her.

When Marcus found out that she was cheating on him with someone else that had money, he realized that she was only about that. He confronted her when he saw a note written to her talking about the good time that she and the other guy had one evening. She became aggressively defensive and blurted out "If you aren't going to focus on me, then I will find someone that will." She packed her bags and was gone that same day. She didn't even take a single picture. He didn't deserve that because he always paid attention to her. His words to her as she stormed down the walkway to her car were "Fine! God help this idiot that you are now with." The guy knew she was married but didn't care so he deserves what will surely be coming his way.

He was pissed so he couldn't help himself

when he blurted out "You are a dumb bitch!" as she slams the car door and drives away. It's a good thing he had her sign an agreement when they met. She must have thought she would be able to change that at some point. Everything remains his. It's the last time he goes out on a date with someone he meets at a coffee house.

After adding things up he realizes he has less than he thought he had. However, that doesn't seem to change his mind. His home is worth around $600,000.00 and the cash reserves equal $700,000.00. Marcus is 49 years of age now and his future is less than certain because he has just come to the conclusion that he does not want to manage people's money anymore. He will stick it out for a while longer until he can come up with a game plan, but right now he has something to take care of. He puts the car in reverse and backs out of the driveway.

A short time later Marcus pulls in front of the homeless shelter and parks. He gets out of the car and puts he hand out as he notices the first snowflakes of the season begin to fall. There is nothing like New York during winter. He enters the shelter and takes a moment to scan the room.

her utility bills from now on, it's almost more than she can stand. She begins to cry and says "God bless you Marcus, you have a good soul," as she hugs him. She then adds "I better go make some more fruit cakes."

Two days later the system is up and running without a hitch. Coming back home from the office, Marcus stops next door to check on things and make sure she is alright. When Mrs. Morgan opens the door this time it's a perfect 72 degrees and it's the first time in ten winters that he has not seen her with a blanket of some kind wrapped around her shoulders. Everything is perfect and he's glad he was able to help her. She is still independent.

It was another tough day at the office. It has been that way for too long now. That deal he was working on the other day fell through because he didn't act in time. It was his first real chance he had to make some money in the last six months. On top of that, many of his clients have seen their portfolios hit very hard despite him moving them to so called "Safer positions." They call him, and for the first time ever, many of them begin to complain that it's his fault. They are used to making money, not losing a lot of it. He has actually lost three clients in the last two weeks. That has never happened before. The whole thing is making him very uneasy.

He is reflecting on things quite a lot as he sits in his kitchen watching the news. Despite being a very intelligent man, if he is looking to feel better about things, watching the news is not the thing to do. However, he watches anyway as he waits five more minutes for his TV dinner to finish cooking in the oven. The broadcaster begins to talk about a local homeless shelter that is going to have to shut its doors because of the lack of funding. "Donations have all but dried up these days," he says. Marcus can't believe his eyes when in the background he notices what looks like the same woman he saw the other day and she appears to still be wearing his coat. His eyes are glued to the set as he sees her sitting down on some portable bed with a young man that is studying.

A sick feeling comes over him as he thinks about that young boy in that situation. There is no way he can live his life like this when that poor boy has to live his life like that. He forgets his dinner in the oven and falls asleep on the couch. The next morning he calls Cheryl at the office and says "I'm sorry. Something else has come up and I won't be able to make it in today. I will see you tomorrow." Cheryl says "No problem," but she is beginning to worry about him because he isn't acting normal. He still has a great big smile everyday and always sounds upbeat but he has never missed work before and all of a sudden he is not showing up that much. As long as the office stays open and she shows up, she will continue to get paid.

She suspects something is wrong with him and she is right. He feels like he let Michelle down because he wasn't there. He had thanked her a million times for everything she had done for him but she was the closest thing to family he had. He feels alone all over again. Marcus is happy to be alive and is in no rush for things to end. If he could live life again and again he would. However, with the way his life has gone, he feels like it's mainly a job. It's a job that he really enjoys. He also believes that his parents are watching and he wants to make them proud of him. His father taught him at an early age to think of others. His father was the best. Nothing in the world was more important than the well being of his beautiful son. Every child deserves a father like Marcus's father was.

As Marcus grabs another coat and heads out the door, it begins to snow. He is happy not to be going to the office and seems to have lost the desire to be there at all. He gets into his car and lets it warm up in the driveway while he grabs a piece of scratch paper from his glove box. He pulls a pen from his jacket and uses the steering wheel as a makeshift desk. He writes down a bunch of dollar amounts including the money spent on the heating system, his modified monthly expenditures, perceived value of his home, his total savings, and other things. It's not like it used to be but he feels that he doesn't need as much as what he thought he would need.

Marcus had always planned on having a wife and a couple of kids. He wanted to be able to provide a good life for them. After ten years of marriage and his wife continually waffling on having kids, the time seems to have passed. Marcus loved his wife and stuck in there until she thought it was the right time for her. It was always going to be the right time for him. It came as a complete shock when she told him that she wanted out because of his constant desire to help others. Most people would have embraced such an idea but for some reason she always had to be the center of attention and when he spent any time thinking of the well being of others, it became a threat to her.

When Marcus found out that she was cheating on him with someone else that had money, he realized that she was only about that. He confronted her when he saw a note written to her talking about the good time that she and the other guy had one evening. She became aggressively defensive and blurted out "If you aren't going to focus on me, then I will find someone that will." She packed her bags and was gone that same day. She didn't even take a single picture. He didn't deserve that because he always paid attention to her. His words to her as she stormed down the walkway to her car were "Fine! God help this idiot that you are now with." The guy knew she was married but didn't care so he deserves what will surely be coming his way.

He was pissed so he couldn't help himself

when he blurted out "You are a dumb bitch!" as she slams the car door and drives away. It's a good thing he had her sign an agreement when they met. She must have thought she would be able to change that at some point. Everything remains his. It's the last time he goes out on a date with someone he meets at a coffee house.

After adding things up he realizes he has less than he thought he had. However, that doesn't seem to change his mind. His home is worth around $600,000.00 and the cash reserves equal $700,000.00. Marcus is 49 years of age now and his future is less than certain because he has just come to the conclusion that he does not want to manage people's money anymore. He will stick it out for a while longer until he can come up with a game plan, but right now he has something to take care of. He puts the car in reverse and backs out of the driveway.

A short time later Marcus pulls in front of the homeless shelter and parks. He gets out of the car and puts he hand out as he notices the first snowflakes of the season begin to fall. There is nothing like New York during winter. He enters the shelter and takes a moment to scan the room.

He notices what looks like an office of some type towards the back of the room. As he slowly walks back there, he notices all the faces of everyone. You can just feel the despair in the air. It's thick like a fog. Everyone must have heard that they are on their last leg at that facility. They are already down on their collective luck and this will surely push many of them over the edge. Marcus knocks on the closed door. The door opens and he enters.

An hour later, Marcus exits the office with a woman that looks like she just won the lottery. She looks at Marcus, shakes his hand and says "God bless you. Thank you so much. Because of you we will be able to stay open and keep some of these people from dying in the cold this winter." Marcus just offered to donate $200,000.00 to the shelter. Not only is he going to donate the money but he is personally going to make sure it is spent wisely and not pocketed by others. He will get with the landlord and pre-pay a couple of year's worth of rent which will total $150,000.00 and will spend the other $50,000.00 on food and supplies. He will take $5,000.00 from that $50,000.00 to lighten and brighten the place up.

They have to feel a sense of hope. A few live plants and a coat of paint will go a long way in lifting spirits. At least he hopes it does.

He has also come to the shelter in search of the woman and the young man he noticed on television. At first, Marcus in unable to locate them and is becoming anxious. Then, all of a sudden, he spots them in another area of the facility. As he walks towards them, the woman looks up and smiles while saying "We meet again." She then leans forward and begins to take the coat off and says "You must have come back for this. Thank you very much for letting me use it. It's nice and warm." She likes that coat.

Marcus is quick to say "No, no. Keep it on, it's yours." She smiles and says "Thank you." He then proceeds to say "I was hoping I can talk to the two of you for a couple minutes if it's alright with you." They agree. Marcus momentarily gets lost in the young man's eyes. Marcus can't help notice his smile, the books all over the bed, and his obvious love for his mother. "It looks like you like to study," says Marcus. The young man, whose name is Darnell, says "Yes sir. I would like to be a doctor one day. I like helping people."

Marcus is moved by the comments of this happy young man. But, how can he possibly be happy when he is living this life?

They all continue to talk for another thirty minutes or so and Marcus finds out why Darnell never knew his father. He took off when he was born. His mother is reluctant to give too many details on what brought them to the shelter. She has a lot of pride. However, when she senses that Marcus is not going to pass judgment, she opens up. "I got hurt and was unable to work. I had no health insurance and next thing you know, here we are with no money except for this. She pulls a wrinkled $20.00 bill out of her pocket and looks at it. Normally, she is a very strong woman but this time she breaks down and begins to cry as she says "I just feel so bad for my son. He doesn't deserve this. He even got accepted to a good University but I don't have any way to let him go.

This kind young soul puts his arms around his mother and says "Don't cry mom, it will be alright. As long as we have each other everything is great." When Marcus hears those words he flashes back to when his mother told him the same thing. He stands back up and says "I have plenty of room at my house. I would like it if you two stay there until we can get him enrolled in college." The woman is confused because she has no idea who Marcus is or that he just offered to donate all that money to the shelter. The last thing she wants to do is to put her son in harm's way.

Just then, the director of the shelter comes back up to him and this time gives him a big hug. "I just had to say thank you one more time," she says. When the woman walks away, Darnell's mother thanks this stranger very much but declines the offer because she believes that there is no way that someone she saw in the street was going to be able to help them out like that. She figured there must be some kind of sinister motive at hand.

Marcus is disappointed but says "I understand. Just one question son. What college is it that accepted you?" Darnell proudly shows him the acceptance letter from UCLA. Marcus says "I just know you are going to be a great doctor. I wish you the best." He pulls out a business card and hands it to Darnell's mother and walks away. Ten days later Darnell and his mother are asked to see the director in her office. His mom has had very few breaks in her life and you can see how nervous she is when walking to the room in the back. She is convinced that she will be told that her and her son's time is up and they will be put out on the street.

When the two of them take a seat, Darnell's mother is taken back when the director hands her a Fed Ex envelope. "What is this?" she asks. The director replies "I have no idea." When she hears that, his mother says "You mean, you aren't kicking us out?" The woman replies "Of course not, you still have up to six months here before you have to find something permanent somewhere else." Darnell's mother nervously opens the strange envelope that is coming from some business in Manhattan.

Darnell keeps asking his mom "What does it say?" before she has a chance to really absorb the words written. "Hold on a minute. I will tell you in a second. Let me read it first," she replies. There are a bunch of different papers and forms in a folder with a cover letter. She begins to shake as she reads it for a second time. It's now the third time she starts to read it and this time it is out loud for Darnell to hear. The letter reads

Dear Darnell,

I enjoyed meeting you and your mother the other day. I think you are both very special people. Your outlook and positive attitude will go a long way in life and your desire to help people should be commended. Whenever someone can be of help to someone else, this is an opportunity that should not be missed. We are all in it together and we all share the same responsibility.

Enclosed is the receipt and paperwork for your tuition. It has been paid for and you will owe nothing in tuition for the entire four years. I also leased and paid for a modest one bedroom apartment only a few blocks away. It is under my name so that it could be a surprise but here are the keys and an agreement signed by me that states how it is for you and your mother to live in. Until your mother is well enough to start working again you may need to also get a job to help out. However, I have also enclosed a check for $15,000.00 to help with books, supplies, some furniture or whatever you two should need. I have also included a couple of train tickets to help get you there. Good luck to you and your mother. I wish you two the best.

Your friend,

Marcus

Darnell's mother can hardly believe it despite reading it three times. Darnell, on the other hand, has absorbed it right away. He begins jumping up and down while yelling "I'm going to college. I'm going to college!" His mother puts her hands together and thanks God above. Her prayers have been answered. They were answered by the man who gave her a coat. Two weeks later, a train pulls into Union Station in Los Angeles. Darnell and his mother walk out of the station to a bright blue sky and a perfect temperature. They have never been to California before. It's the first day of their new lives. They stop there for a moment taking it all in and then get into a taxi. The driver asks "Where to?" Darnell's mother proudly says "The UCLA college campus in West Los Angeles please." Off they go, to a brighter tomorrow.

Meanwhile, back in New York, Marcus has brought himself back to work with the knowledge that he now wants to do something different with his life. Until he figures out exactly what that is,

33

he will go through the motions but be very conservative in his investment strategy. He doesn't want to get anymore phone calls from people who are losing so much of their security. Without a doubt, this new style will slow his business down to a crawl. He has normally been the guy who makes quick moves and has made many of his clients a lot of money. However, with that approach came some pretty big loses too. The difference was that when the market was speculative he almost always had a move to offset any loss. These days, the speculative play is not there for the most part.

Again, he sits in his chair that he has turned to face the window and stares down below. It seems as though that each time he does that he gets lost in thought. This time he thinks for a moment about the woman that works in the grocery store that he shops at. He has never been bold enough to ask her out or see if she is married, but something is moving him to gather the courage to do so. After all, she is very nice and good looking on top of it. Margaret also seems to flirt with him a little each time. It's nothing big, just little winks or extra long smiles but it's enough for him to think that he may actually have a shot this time. Marcus doesn't even know what he is looking for, he just feels lonely.

As the workday comes to an end, Marcus puts on his other winter coat, grabs his briefcase, and says "Good bye. I'll see you tomorrow," to his secretary. He heads towards the subway. As he makes his way through the congested streets he looks down for a moment and accidently bumps the shoulder of another man as they cross the intersection. "Excuse me. I'm sorry," says Marcus as he looks up. The man looks at Marcus and says "No problem." as he continues on. Marcus looks at the man as he passes and notices how he is holding the hand of a young person around the age of five or six. The other hand of the child is also being held by a woman.

Marcus forgets for a moment that he has yet to finish crossing the street and stops in his tracks to stare at this loving family as they go on their way. He flashes back to when his parents were walking him over to his friend's house just before they were killed. Just then, a car blasts its horn and comes to a screeching halt just inches away from Marcus's legs. "What the hell are you doing?" yells a man as he sticks his head out the window. Marcus steps out of the way and the man peels off. He has learned to deal with it, yet at this moment, he feels sad that he never had children. Marcus wanted to be the kind of man his dad was.

Continuing to make his way to the subway, Marcus stops in front of the homeless man that always hangs out in front of the church. The guy never asks anyone for anything as people walk by. The only thing he has ever said to Marcus is "Have a blessed day."

When you see the same homeless person nearly every day, it hits you in a different way. To watch the slow erosion of a body and mind gets to him. This one is especially hard because it's an older guy who clearly isn't going to have anyone come knocking on his door. As Marcus walks up to him, the man breaks from the norm and says "How are you doing this evening?" Marcus walks up a couple of steps, pulls his coat together at the middle and asks the man to come with him. The old frail man easily agrees and attempts to gather his few things. He has no idea where he is going but he is happy someone asks him to go anywhere. Marcus stops him and says "I'll carry it for you my friend."

With that, Marcus and the man walk a few blocks to the subway. Along the way the man says "Do you mind if I ask where we are going?" Marcus replies by saying "You are going home." The old man is shocked and smiles from ear to ear. He thinks for sure he is going to be taken to Marcus's place. After a thirty minute ride on the subway they walk a couple more blocks towards the Market near Marcus's house. For the longest time he has passed a furnished single apartment for rent just across from the market.

It's not for rent any longer. Marcus meets with the manager and tells her that he will be paying for this gentleman to live there. She says "Alright, that will require first, last, and a security deposit." Out comes Marcus's check book with a dwindling balance. With the stroke of a pen the man is then handed the keys to his new place. The old man drops his few bags, hugs Marcus, and begins to cry. "God bless you son!" he says. One last task and Marcus is going to go home. The guy needs to eat so he says "I'll be back in about 20 minutes. I'm going to get something to eat." It's hard to know if the man even heard him because he is in such a state of trance as he stands in the middle of the room just staring at stuff. With Marcus now gone, the man snaps out of it and he thinks he remembers Marcus saying something about food. Boy! That too is good news to him because he has not eaten in two days. A couple of the shelters he had been eating at ran out of food. The donations are few and far between these days.

Minutes later, Marcus returns with the woman that he likes from the Market. She happily agreed to help carry some things over for the man. Five big bags of groceries are put onto the kitchen table and the man nearly dies of a heart attack right there. He needs to sit down and catch his breath. This is the first time in 10 years he has had a place to call his own. "The man is so spent that he actually pushes some of the items away and says "I can't. I will never be able to pay you back." Marcus quickly replies by saying "You already have." Marcus also made arrangements for the market to supply the man with what he needs and they are to send the bill directly to him.

This is just the place where Marcus finds himself now. He is completely unmotivated to go forward with his current business. The idea of stepping into someone's life at a time when they desperately need it and help in some small way is when he feels happiest with life. Otherwise, he often feels it's a cruel place that feels more like a place to prove oneself. He just wants to go home to his parents.

As Marcus and the woman walk back to the market he gathers the courage to stop on the sidewalk and ask her out. "Thank you very much for helping Margaret. I notice you don't have a wedding ring. I was wondering if you would like to go out to dinner sometime?" he asks. "I'm sorry Marcus. You are very sweet for asking. I am married. I just don't wear the ring because I keep messing it up at work. Plus, he knows I am true to him." Of course Marcus is disappointed to get another rejection. Well, perhaps it's not a rejection but it is still a no either way. No point in thinking about her at night anymore. Marcus is tired and decides to head home.

On the subway ride home he settles into a seat and can't help but notice the faces of many of the people standing or sitting. There are a few that look to be happy or at peace but the vast majority have some kind of pain or distress written on their faces. There are also some that appear to have lost the battle and are just ridding the subway to keep warm because there is no other place for them to go. It's a bit too much for Marcus to take in this tired state that he is in. He leans forward and puts his face in his hands. Marcus wishes he can help everyone.

After only a few seconds in this position, Marcus feels a hand on his shoulder. He is taken off guard because there are many seats available all around him. It's kind of late at night and this subway car is only half full. Just a few seconds ago he had nobody sitting within eight or ten seats from him and they haven't stopped in the twenty seconds his head was down. He looks up to see a man. Well groomed and of Latin decent he speaks softly while looking at Marcus in the eyes. His hand remains on Marcus's shoulder. "You can't save them all," the stranger says.

Marcus has no idea who this person is and

doesn't remember seeing him moments ago but he feels at ease next to him. The man continues by saying "I know you want to, but don't feel bad for those you can't help or choose not to. Feel happy for all those that you have. You have done far more than most and you need to take care of yourself." Marcus looks at him with the innocence of a young boy and says "My name is Marcus." The young man responds by saying "I know. My name is Nathan." They shake hands and Nathan gets up and walks back to the front of the car. A minute later Marcus gets up because he wants to thank Nathan but he is unable to locate him. It is very odd because there is nowhere this person could have gone other than the front of the car. It's like he got in front of the other passengers that were standing up and vanished. Marcus is too tired to think about it much and just goes back to his seat and continues on his way home.

Chapter 2

One month later, Marcus is at the office boxing up his last few things. He gave his faithful secretary another $4,000.00 and told her last week that he was shutting down. It didn't come as a surprise because he began mentioning it quite a while ago. Now he stands in his empty office, which he had for a decade, and stares out the window to the street below one last time. He then turns to the last item which is an old picture of him and Michelle. He gently removes it from the wall and places it in the box. With that, he puts the box under his arm and closes the door behind him for good.

Marcus has not come up with a solid plan as of yet. That by itself is very much out of character for him because he has just left a career that was all about planning. He had to be able to make quick moves and fast decisions. But those decisions and moves were all well thought out plans that were created at a much earlier time. If scenario #2 came to life then he would simply put plan B into action.

It's half full or half empty but it is seldom one of them 100% of the time. The energy it takes to be the eternal optimist is usually more than the average person has to offer. Luckily for Marcus, he was born with that kind of energy and spirit. His reserve tanks alone could power another individual's life for a long time. Yet, with this advantage, he considers himself to not have luck on his side. It feels like it is a constant struggle, a constant battle with few winners.

Perhaps he has a restless spirit that just doesn't know how to rest or it might be that there is just a key ingredient missing. Either way, he longs to feel complete. It's now time to leave this part of his life behind and change courses.

This Monday morning Marcus is not quite sure what to do with himself. It feels good not having to go to the office but he kind of wants to go out and do something. It's just so that he can say "I went out and did something" to himself. It's not like he has to start collecting a paycheck tomorrow but it would not be a bad idea to figure out a way to make money pretty soon. He has been going through it much faster than before.

Ever since he came to the conclusion that he would not be having kids, his drive to make money and create a future for them is no more. He is not driven whatsoever to gain wealth to serve his own needs but it has always been about surviving and prospering enough to take care of others especially if he had anything to do with bringing them into this world. He likes the idea of being there on a constant basis to serve as a guide, a tutor, a friend, and a nurturing father type to a young person, a child.

The weather has improved considerably and it's actually a nice day in New York. The sun shines brightly without a cloud in sight as Marcus leaves the building for the last time. It seems to be kind of fitting. He is going to walk extra far today and get off a stop earlier on his way home. It feels so nice out and he is not headed anywhere but home to be by himself. He finds the perfect place to stop. It's a local coffee spot complete with atmosphere and vibe. A nice cup of coffee should hit the spot.

A cozy spot in the corner listening to some Motown playing in the background should surely help relax him. After a few deep breaths, he quickly accepts his new non directional approach. It feels good. Up until now, he has been second guessing himself. Just then, as if someone was saying "Hey, wait a minute, not so fast!" he notices a struggle outside. Some guy is trying to force a young girl into a car. At this time, there aren't many people in the coffee shop or outside to notice it. However, Marcus does and in an instant he jumps out of his seat and runs out the door. He spills his coffee all over the floor. He also knocks over his box of items. As if it were in slow motion, the glass in the picture of him and Michelle breaks.

The assailant is so preoccupied with what he is doing that as soon as Marcus is up on him he is still pulling on the girl's arm in an attempt to pull her into the car. Marcus yells "Stop! What the hell are you doing?" to the guy as he bends over and tries to get between them. Marcus doesn't notice the knife in his other hand and isn't fast enough to get out of the way as the guy pushes the knife into Marcus's side. Before Marcus falls to the ground, he looks at the knife in his side and gathers all the strength he can. He manages to summon enough to deliver a thunderous punch to the guy's mouth, knocking out some of his front teeth. That was enough to stop everything in its tracks. The man lets go of the girl and with a bloody mouth leans back into the driver's seat and floors it. The tires screech as he takes off. Marcus falls backwards onto the sidewalk and loses consciousness. The girl runs over to the coffee shop to get help. She yells "Call 911. Someone has been stabbed." to the guy bent over cleaning the mess on the floor.

At the hospital it's questionable for a while but the surgeons are able to save Marcus's life. He lay in the hospital bed with nobody by his side. There is no next of kin. There are no real close friends he wants to bother. What for? A week later he is released from the hospital. His side is still sore so he holds it as he walks and makes his way to the closest subway station. He finally makes it to his front door. Good thing he has no pets. They would have had a problem.

Before he is able to make it inside, he notices the daughter of his elderly neighbor coming out of the house and she too is caring a small box. "I haven't seen you in a while. How have you been?" Marcus asks. With a tear rolling down her face the woman says "I don't think you heard, but my mother died last week." Marcus puts his box down and walks over to her and gives her a big hug and softly says "No, I didn't. I'm so sorry. She was a great woman. I will miss her." Marcus then goes on to tell her that if she needs anything to go ahead and call him.

Marcus immediately sits down in his favorite chair as he enters the house. He holds his side because the walking, even though it was slow, was too ambitious. He should have taken a taxi. An hour goes by and he is still sitting there. She was an older woman but Marcus became close to Mrs. Morgan and the news hurts more than his physical injury. Together they form a mighty one two combination. It has him down for the count. But just then, Marcus takes a deep breath, puts both hands on the arm rests and pushes himself up and out of the chair.

In the kitchen, he makes himself a cup of coffee and something to eat. He turns on the small television set that sits on the counter. He is too tired to pay attention to what the newscaster is saying. They are doing a story on the local homeless shelter that was able to keep it doors open because of the generosity of one person that wished to remain anonymous. But the story doesn't just end there. The main part of the story is about a freshman UCLA student that risked his own life and saved an elderly couple from certain death.

Just two days earlier, the student was walking to campus when he noticed an overturned car on a side street. A small crowd had gathered to witness the car in flames. Without a second's hesitation, the young man had let go of his backpack and ran over to the car despite the inherent risk and bent over to see if anyone was inside and if they were still alive. Sure enough, there was an elderly couple that had survived up until that point. He quickly unbuckled the seatbelt of the woman passenger and pulled her out of the burning car and placed her to the sidewalk for the others to tend to her.

People had called 911 and the sirens can be heard in the distance. However, there was no time to waste. The young man ran back to the car to get the male driver. This time he struggled greatly in trying to undo the man's seatbelt. The student desperately looked around for something to cut the seatbelt with. The quick thinker that he is, the young student took his shirt off, wrapped it around his hand and grabbed a large piece of broken glass from the side view mirror and feverishly began to rub the edge on the belt. The shirt helped but he cut his hand over and over and blood dripped on the elder man's shirt. With one last forward motion the seatbelt was cut in half and the man is pulled out and dragged next to his wife. As soon as the elder man's head gently rested on the grass, the car blew up in a massive fireball as the fire engine is seen approaching in the background.

While the paramedics began to work on the victims, the crowd, that had grown larger, circled around the student and began to praise his efforts. Everyone put their arms around him at some point and a chant of "Hero, Hero, Hero" grew. Marcus finally turns toward the television at the very end of the segment. He is stunned to see Darnell, the young man he helped, being interviewed. Marcus quickly reaches and grabs the control to turn up the volume. At that exact moment Darnell is seen reaching in his pocket and pulling out a business card.

The female reporter repeats her question. "Darnell, what gave you the courage to help those people like that?" she asks. Darnell looks at the card and holds it up right in front of the camera. The card reads Marcus K. Mather. "This man," he says. Of course, it is his mother that raised him and she is the greatest contributor to him being who he is. But this time, the man that rescued them is being thanked. Darnell then looks directly in the camera and says "Please, I have been trying to reach this man and I don't know where he is. If anyone out there knows him please ask him to call the Administration office at U.C.L.A. I want to thank him again for helping us out."

The reporter then hits him with one last question. "Is that your father?" she asks. "No, but I wish he was. It's a gentleman who saved two people that he didn't even know." The reporter finishes by saying "What a great story. Good luck Darnell. We all wish you well." The segment then ends and the anchor moves on to other news.

Marcus can hardly believe his eyes or ears. It's too bad that he only heard that part and missed the story. Marcus does not know to be happy because he doesn't know what happened.

He just caught the part where Darnell was asking for help finding him and he noticed the bandages wrapped around the young man's hand. It's now evening and the University office is closed but he grabs his cell phone and leaves a heartfelt message and plea for someone to give Darnell his contact info. He is worried the young man is in trouble and needs his help.

The next morning, Marcus gets a call from Darnell and he lets out a huge sigh of relief when hearing that he is fine. Darnell proudly recounts what happened in detail. They had only met the one time when Marcus came into the shelter but you would never know it from the enthusiasm in which he speaks to Marcus. It's as if a son was looking for praise from his father. Marcus is stunned to hear what had taken place and his chest swells with pride and joy. Marcus says "Great job son. I'm proud of you. You are one hell of a man!"

Even though he has a wonderful mother who sacrifices everything for him, Darnell has never in his life had anyone that represented a father type figure. His mother doesn't date and spends all her time trying her best to be there for her son. She is in a wheelchair. Not once in his life has Darnell been embarrassed of his mother. He takes care of her like she takes care of him. He pushes her around with pride. She is all he has. Marcus hangs up the phone after a ten minute conversation and is more pleased that he has ever been in his life. The moment when Darnell said "Thank you for saving me and my mom, I think of you as my dad," will echo in his ears for the rest of his life. At last, he finally feels like he has made a real difference. He has been making a difference for a long time but this is the first time he actually feels it.

Over the course of the next few days Marcus really doesn't do too much. He over did it the day he was released and now just wants to sit back and relax for a while. For now, he is content with going to the local coffee spot and reading the newspaper while sipping on coffee. Sure enough, this morning he opens the paper and there is the story of Darnell's heroics complete with picture. He reads it over and over and then gently folds up the article, saving it, and tosses the rest of the paper in the common use basket. Back home, he trims up the article, puts it in a frame and hangs it on the wall.

The next day, Marcus is back at the same coffee house at the same time and in the same spot. He does like the freedom he now has but he also likes a sense of routine as well. He likes sitting next to the window to watch all that goes on outside. In the smallest of ways it takes the edge off of being alone. His mind begins to wonder and he just stares off into space as he thinks about Darnell and his mother. In many ways they have so much more than he does. They have each other and no amount of money on earth can buy the same quality of love that you get from a genuine love. To him, that is a love that exists even when financial security has not been achieved yet or it has taken a big hit. A sense of "Team" is very important to him. He wants to succeed together and fail together. And if together, they will never lose. He thinks of how hard it must be on the both of them.

Just then, a tapping on the window wakes him out of his dream like state. It's a woman he knows. She's the best friend of his former secretary. He motions for her to come inside. As she comes to the table, he gets up to give her a hug. She notices him grimace and grab his side in pain. "What happened to you?" she asks. "It's no big deal. I just had a little accident," he replies. They proceed to engage in small talk for a few minutes until he asks about Cheryl.

When he hears about how his long time friend Cheryl, her husband, and their kids are losing their house and have no place to go, he becomes visibly tense. Not mad, just stressed. This economy is just ruthless and the number of victims is just too large to calculate. It's the end of the middle class as we knew it. Just then, the woman says "Well, I better get going." She gives him a gentle hug and walks out the door. He could have done without hearing that. But he did and will most probably attempt to do something about it.

Normally, Marcus would have left by now but he continues to hang out. It's not like he needs to be anywhere. He has nobody waiting for him. He gets up and grabs a couple of napkins off the counter. Pulling a pen from his breast pocket of his blazer he begins to do a little math. He is very good with numbers and it takes him just a couple of minutes to evaluate his total financial condition. The new numbers he has come up with are startling. The dramatic decrease in wealth, due to his giving, has put him in a precarious position. Yet, for some odd reason, he is not terrified. He continues to analyze and predict his future needs given the certainties that face him.

After a few moments of deep thought Marcus gets up, crumples up the napkins, and places them in the trash. By his calculations, he has just enough money left for one last grand gesture. He is too tired to do anything about it tonight but come tomorrow a few lives will change forever.

In the morning, Marcus gets in his car and drives a few short miles to where Cheryl and the rest of her family have been living. He is lucky to have left when he did because he gets there right at the moment when Cheryl's husband is closing the back of the moving truck. Cheryl is in the front yard with her arm around the kids looking at and saying goodbye to their house.

Everyone is surprised to see a car pull into the driveway and directly in front of the moving truck. They are even more surprised when they see Marcus get out of the car. Marcus gets out and walks over where the entire family has gathered. Cheryl is quick to give him a hug while saying "Oh my goodness Marcus, what are you doing here?" Her husband reaches his hand out to shake Marcus's hand. Marcus responds by saying "I heard what is happening." Before he is done with the sentence, Cheryl breaks into tears.

"Where are you going to go?" asks Marcus. Her husband Ron answers. "We don't really know where. Because we are both unemployed now, we have little money. We really just have enough for some food. We are going to go stay with her parents for as short of a time as possible. I can't believe it. We have worked so hard for so long and it has come to this. But at least we have each other," he says while hugging his wife. Cheryl looks into his eyes, smiles, and kisses him. Then they both look down at their young children and bring them in for a group hug. Cheryl then says something that Marcus will never forget. "As long as we all have each other, life is good," she says.

Marcus automatically flashes back to his youth and when his mother said that to him for the last time. There is no question as to what he feels he must do. He pulls out a spare set of keys from his pocket and places them in Ron's hand. He wants Ron to feel like he is still providing for his family. "What's this?" Ron asks. "Your new home," replies Marcus. Cheryl lets go of Ron's other hand, puts her hands over her mouth and begins to cry like she has never cried before. It's as if every pent up emotion and worry she has ever had came rushing out. When the kids hear the news they begin to jump up and down for joy. They even give each other a high five. The family is so overwhelmed that they don't even ask a single question at that time. They just do what Marcus asks. "You two follow me in the truck and the kids can come with me," he says. He then gets in the car and rolls down the window and says "It's 189 Harrington lane."

Even though Marcus has been over to their house a few times before, they have never been over to his house. Harrington Lane is a well known street in the area so Marcus isn't concerned with them not being able to find the place. Marcus is very conscious of creating memories and he can just imagine the memory that is being created inside the cab of the truck.

As he pulls the big truck out of the driveway, Ron is just so excited that he slaps the steering wheel and says "Yes! I told you baby, everything will work out." The truth of the matter is that Ron had a hard time convincing himself of that but had to keep saying it to be strong for the family. Cheryl knows all about Marcus and his generosity but she is struggling to understand what he means. "What do you think he means?" she asks. Driving down the road without knowing where you are going is an odd feeling and one that the two of them are enjoying at the moment.

Harrington Lane goes from a main street in town to a beautiful residential neighborhood at the end of it. After a few minutes, Ron and Cheryl lose Marcus and the kids in traffic. When the couple gets close enough they slow down to look for the correct address. Well, sure enough, they are able to find the house. It's because they spotted Marcus's car in the driveway and the kids jumping up and down, while waving their hands, in order to signal their parents.

Both Ron & Cheryl look at each other. "Boy!

this is a nice place," says Cheryl. It's not a mansion. In fact, it's a fairly modest 3 bedroom home but very well kept. "He must live here. That is so generous to let us stay here like this," says Ron. At this point, they feel that their prayers have been answered. As they get out of the truck the kids come and grab their mother's hand and pull her inside to look around. "Mom, mom, he said this is going to be my room," says one of the kids. Cheryl pokes her head in the room and says "Wow that is nice. Your very own room, do you believe it?" The other child is quick to grab her arm once again and pull her over to the room next door. "He said this one is going to be mine mom," says the other child. "Wow, you two sure are lucky," she says.

Meanwhile, Marcus and Ron remain in the front yard looking at the house. Ron looks over at Marcus and says "I can't believe you are going to let us stay with you at your house. I promise, we won't be a bother." Marcus puts his hand on Ron's back and says "Let's go inside. I want to talk to you two about that."

Marcus was quick thinking and had already set the kids up with a good movie that they have not even seen. It's amazing how quickly some kids are able to adapt. In the short 15 minutes that they have been there, they have already gone into the refrigerator to help themselves to something to drink. After all, they were just told "Get comfortable and treat this place like your home."

The three adults sit around the kitchen table with a glass of wine in hand. "I can't believe you are letting us stay with you like this Marcus," says Cheryl. "I'm not just letting you stay here. I am giving you the house," says Marcus. Cheryl begins to tremble in shock. "You are doing what?" she asks. "I'm signing over my house to you. It's all paid for. You will never have to worry about having a place for the family anymore."

It's clear that Cheryl is way beyond her emotional limits and she blacks out for a moment and begins to fall off the chair but her husband is there to catch her. While trying to bring her to, Ron turns to Marcus and says "You can't do that. What are you going to do? Where are you going to go?" Cheryl comes back around and throws her arms around Marcus. Over the course of the next two weeks Marcus will stay on the couch in the living room until all the arrangements can be made. After everyone else has turned in, Marcus is on the couch watching television with the volume on low. He can't help but feel envious of the family he sees before him. Unconditional love and support have now completely filled the air inside this house. What a great feeling.

Just then, Cheryl appears and joins him on the couch. She puts her hand on his leg in a friendly way and says "You can't do this. This is your home that you worked for and deserve." Marcus looks at her and says in a calm, slow, comforting voice "I know but we are talking about the well being of four people versus one person. The kids need security and I want them to enjoy being kids. "Where do you plan on going?" she asks. "I think I'm heading to California," Marcus replies.

Two weeks later, Marcus finds himself on a plane heading to the west coast. All his furniture and bulky items have been placed in the garage and will remain there for an undetermined length of time. They can stay there forever if he wants them to. However, he has taken a box of essentials. It's his box of memories. A couple large suitcases of clothes and 1 medium box of memories is all he is taking to start his new life. Marcus has done very little traveling and can only remember taking a plane one other time. He managed to grab a window seat and he stares out the window before takeoff. It would terrify most people of Marcus's age to leave the known and deal with the uncertainty and this self imposed insecurity. To have the level of financial security that Marcus had is the dream of many. Most people would think he lost his mind. The fact is, he found his soul.

As he sips orange juice from his little clear plastic cup filled with too much ice, Marcus pulls out his check book from the inside breast pocket of his suit jacket and takes a quick glance at his balance. He has cleared all stock positions and holdings a long time ago. He has been maintaining a purely cash position ever since. He adds his checking to his savings and comes up with a startling figure. Even he takes a second look at it. He will need to start bringing some money in soon. It doesn't have to be anything like before but something coming in at this stage is of huge importance. Not for a second does he regret anything he has done. He hasn't thought to himself how he shouldn't have helped a certain individual. However, he does realize that he has to survive to be helpful. It's time to buckle down.

Hours pass and the Captain of the plane is heard over the speaker saying "We are making our final approach. On behalf of the crew and I, we want to thank you for flying with us and welcome to Los Angeles. The weather is a perfect 72 degrees with clear skies. Enjoy your stay."

After retrieving his bags from the baggage pick up area, Marcus makes his way outside to grab a taxi. As the cab driver gets out of the car and puts Marcus's bags in the trunk, he turns towards Marcus and says "Where to sir?" Marcus tells him the location of a hotel in the Westwood Village part of West Los Angeles. "It's right near the UCLA college campus," says Marcus. "Oh sure, I know where that is," says the gentleman.

The plan Marcus has come up with is to stay at a hotel for a week or two. And while doing so, he will find an apartment to rent. He didn't want to obligate himself to anything online without getting a true feel for it first. As the cab driver takes a slightly longer way than necessary, Marcus stares out the window and soaks in his new surroundings. "Boy, it sure is different than New York," he says to the driver. "That's for sure," replies the driver in a thick East Indian accent.

Nearly an hour later Marcus is dropped off in front of the hotel. Traffic was bad. He gives the driver a nice tip and off he goes. Once Marcus gets settled in his room he makes his way downstairs to the hotel restaurant. He wastes no time and locates a newspaper in the lobby and takes it with him. As he eats dinner, he pulls a pen from his jacket pocket and circles a couple of places that he wants to check out. They are in an area called Brentwood.

After the conversation he had with Darnell, Marcus wants to be closer in both heart and location. There was nothing holding him down in New York and everything there seemed to be the same as the days and years before. Marcus was able to hear in Darnell's voice that he longed for that fatherly figure he never had. Even if they never see each other, Marcus wants

Darnell to know that he is close by. And who knows, maybe Marcus will find a woman to love him as he loves her.

The next day Marcus arrives at the first location circled. It's a modest one bedroom apartment with a balcony and a pool. It's a far cry from the space and tranquility that came from his house he just gave away. But he likes it nonetheless and just like that a one year lease is signed and he is allowed to move in as early as the following week. If he doesn't like it after a while he can always move next year.

Since he managed to get that done rather quickly he slowly walks the 3 miles back towards Westwood Village and the UCLA campus. Once he gets there, he asks some students that are walking with backpacks "Could you tell me where the administration office is?" They happily point in the direction and give him details on how to get there. "Thank you very much," he says.

Once he finds the place, Marcus enters and asks about Darnell. "Could you tell me where his classes are located?" he asks the woman. Unaware of Darnell's recent celebrity status of sorts and not knowing who Marcus is, she is not ready to make an exception. "I'm sorry sir; we can't give out that information. It's policy," she says. Out of sheer coincidence, a classmate of Darnell happens to be in the office dealing with some paperwork. He waits until Marcus leaves and follows him outside. "Excuse me," he says. Marcus turns around. "You were asking about Darnell?" asks the student. "Yes I was. Do you know where I can find him?" Marcus asks. Before the student gives him any information he asks Marcus "Are you that gentleman he mentioned in the news segment?" Marcus says "Yes. I am hoping to surprise him." With a smile, the student puts his hand out to shake. "That is a real nice thing you did for him. I'm Andrew. I have a couple of courses with him. He plays on the basketball team and there is a game at the Pavilion tonight. Maybe you can catch him there," he says.

Marcus is very surprised to hear this news. Darnell never mentioned anything about it, nor did he read anything about that in the article. "I would love to go. Where can I buy a ticket?" asks Marcus. Andrew points in the direction of the Pavilion and says "I do have to warn you, Darnell does not play very much. He normally sits on the bench. He told me that he made the team because the coach said 'he has never seen anyone hustle as much.' It's too bad they don't play him because he is pretty good." The young man does give Marcus the times and locations of the two classes he has with Darnell.

California seems to be good to Marcus so far. "I think I am going to like it here," he says out loud as he walks to the ticket office. Full of confidence, Marcus speaks to the person behind the counter. "Yes you can help me, thank you. I would like to buy a ticket to tonight's game," he says. "I'm sorry but tonight's game has been totally sold out for a long time," replies the student worker. "Ah man, thanks anyway," says a slightly dejected Marcus as he turns and heads back from where he came.

Incredibly, Marcus's day still holds some surprises. Knowing that the game has been sold out for quite some time, a scalper hangs out close by. He's good. It's just another student sitting on a brick wall studying from a text book that casually says "I got a ticket for tonight's game." to Marcus as he passes in front of him. Marcus isn't going to pass judgment. He just wants to go to tonight's game. He wouldn't even mind if they were the worst seats in the house, he just feels like being there.

"How much?" asks Marcus as he looks around to make sure it's not some kind of "Sting Operation." After all, he has spent most of his life in New York so he is street smart as well. "Five hundred and fifty," replies the young student scalper. "Ouch!" mumbles Marcus. The young man looks at Marcus and shows him the seat location. "Best seat in the house. A little courtside action," remarks the apparent chemistry student. And just like that, the deal is done and Marcus pulls out the cash in his pocket. He peels away $550 from the $700.00 he had with him. He can't get over how expensive that ticket was but he is as excited as can be to finally see the young man that he only met once before.

The sudden and unexpected seems to continue to dominate Marcus's life as of late. Between getting stabbed and all of the changes that keep occurring, Marcus is beginning to slow down. It's not like he is that old but he is not that young either. The endless amount of energy that seems to have been with him his throughout life doesn't seem that endless anymore. Yet, he continues to keep going.

When Marcus finally makes his way back to the hotel to rest and get ready for the big game later that night, he sits and looks out the window to the street below. On the hotel writing pad that is so generously provided by the $175.00 a night hotel, Marcus calculates his money situation yet again. It is at a mere fraction of the money he had not even a year ago. He has enough money now to pay the rent for a year, furnish it modestly and buy a modest car in cash. He gave the other to Cheryl. He feels the pressure now and picks up the paper off the table and opens it to the Want Ads. He pulls his pen from his jacket pocket and circles the job opportunities right for him. He can hardly believe how few positions are open. For most of his life he has been managing money for others but now he refuses to do it anymore and has little money left to manage for himself. Smaller amounts of money have a tendency to be self managing. It's usually need driven.

To others, Marcus has failed to plan properly for his future. If he were to have just held onto his money and not done what he has over the last year he would have been set. He could have just lived out the rest of his life in his paid for home. Instead, he has opted to help those that he can in whatever way he could. He decided to relieve some of their burdens and make it harder for himself. It's a huge gamble to say the least.

Meanwhile, back in New York, the family he helped save is adjusting quite well. They kept many of Marcus's furnishings in the house to pay tribute and serve as a constant reminder. Plus, they are nice things. They have painted the inside to give it that new house smell and feel while doing some small things like turn the kids' rooms into rooms for kids. Cheryl washes the dishes while the music from the radio plays softly in the background. Her husband bursts into the kitchen with great news. "I got the job," he says in an extremely animated fashion. It's complete with fist pumping. Cheryl turns off the water, dries her hand on a towel and gives him a huge hug while saying "Oh honey, that is just great. I knew you could do it." A tear of joy rolls down Ron's face as he hugs his wife. It has been so stressful with

70

the economy being so bad. He finally feels like a man again, a provider.

Without question he knows there is more to being a man than bringing home money and women provide just as much and sometimes more. But, to go for so long and not contribute because of his inability to find work made him feel less than one. "I was afraid you would leave me or something," says Ron. Cheryl looks at him as if she is angry and says "Don't be stupid. I would never leave you. It's not like you didn't try. And remember, it's for better or worse. I don't remember the preacher saying 'Stick around for the good, but if it gets bad or times gets hard, you are not a team anymore and it's okay to go.' Do you?" A relieved Ron looks at her and says "No."

At the shelter, things are also going well. Ever since Marcus made that large donation, others have followed suit and they are now well funded for the foreseeable future. The old man that was homeless sits and watches television while eating something warm he prepared. He feels like a millionaire. The woman he saved from the attacker still has nightmares but she is alive and will eventually forget all about it.

Marcus looks in the mirror while tying a not in his tie. He has always liked to dress nicely. It's not that he goes out and spends a fortune on clothes but he has a sense of style and knows how to put things together. If he is not at home, he feels uncomfortable if his is not wearing a suit or at least a sport coat. He never bought into the whole idea of corporate casual. Marcus believes that casual Fridays are less professional Fridays.

After a few adjustments to his jacket, Marcus picks up the phone and calls downstairs for the hotel to arrange a taxi to pick him up and take him to the game. He can't deal with another walk of more than a mile. He has done way too much as it is. He is very excited to be going to the game. This is the moment he has been waiting for, the chance to surprise Darnell by just being there when he walks out of class or, in this case, when the team finishes playing their game.

When Marcus exits the hotel, on the way to the waiting taxi, he is struck by how different the cabs are here compared to those of New York. The one picking him up from the airport seemed normal because it was the standard yellow taxi color that you see everywhere. But this one looks like someone's personal vehicle that they converted into a taxi. Marcus bends down and gets in the backseat. Marcus tells the driver where he wants to go and off they go. "Is this your own car?" asks Marcus. The driver turns his head around to answer. "Yes it is," replies the man. "Do you mind if I ask you, do you make decent money?" asks Marcus. Nobody has ever inquired or shown any kind of interest like this before so the driver is actually happy that someone asked something about himself. "Some days I do pretty well," answers the man.

Just a few short minutes later, the taxi pulls into the UCLA campus and out climbs Marcus. "That will be ten dollars," says the driver. Marcus reaches in his pocket and pulls out a twenty dollar bill, hands it to him and says "Keep the change." With a smile, the driver says "Thank you very much sir." It's been a long time since Marcus has felt so good, so energized. In the cab he was feeling worn down but when he steps out and begins walking towards the gymnasium he gets a second wind. Not only does he really enjoy watching basketball on any level, but he is just so excited to see Darnell that he can barely stand it.

Anyone being helped at any stage of their life brings a great deal of satisfaction to Marcus but to help a young person with a world of potential and a heart of gold makes Marcus feel as though his life has meaning. It was the phone conversation he had with Darnell that made him finally feel that way. It may also be that for a moment, he felt like a dad.

Marcus has never been to a college game and is taken back by how many people are also making their way to the Pavilion. The energy is electric around the venue and when he finally makes his way inside and to his seat he is glad to see that he is close to the action. As he sits down his hopes begin to fade about the idea of being able to catch the attention of Darnell who will surely be caught up in the crowd afterward. It's a bit disappointing because Marcus had built up this moment in his head where the Bruins win the big game and he and Darnell lock eyes immediately following the game winning shot and Darnell comes running over. That happens to Marcus quite a bit. Even though he has learned to have modest expectations regarding everything, he still can't help picturing the perfect scenario in his

74

head. He is a doer and a dreamer.

Since he is nice and early, Marcus decides to get up and grab a cup of coffee before the players come out for their warm-ups. Making his way through the crowd he finds a place selling coffee. When he sees the number of people in line he is tempted to forget it and go back to his seat but decides to stick it out. It's mainly because the person in front of him is a nicely dressed African American woman in her mid forties. He can't tell if she is pretty or not, but she sure does look good from the back. And the fragrance she is wearing is something he doesn't remember ever smelling before. It's got him in a brief trance.

As the woman picks up her extra hot Mocha she moves the wrong way and accidently turns directly into the chest of Marcus. "Oh my goodness, I'm so sorry!" she says as her drink spills onto Marcus's jacket. Marcus doesn't even look down to see the extent of the damage. He is stunned to see the face of an angel. She looks so sweet. He actually has a hard time spitting out any words for a few seconds and then finally responds by saying "Oh, that's alright. Don't worry about it."

Like a true gentleman, he doesn't want to make her feel bad for an accident and takes off his jacket while ordering a cup of coffee for himself and mocha for her. "You don't need to do that," she says. "I want to," he replies. "You are so sweet," she says while standing on her toes to give him a peck on the cheek. He is a fairly tall guy standing at 6'4". With all the unforeseen things that happen in life, this is one that he wasn't expecting at all, especially since she seems to have taken an immediate liking to him.

Normally not so bold, the slightly embarrassed but smiling woman reaches in her purse and pulls out a business card and places it in Marcus's shirt pocket. "Call me sometime," she says. A few seconds earlier she managed to notice that he didn't have a wedding ring on. Caught up in the moment, Marcus forgets to glance at her hand and replies by saying "I certainly will."

That stain will never come out and he knows it but could care less and instead of lugging it around for the entire evening, he pulls everything he needs out of his pockets and places the coat in a nearby trash can. The game is just about to start so he hustles back to his seat just in time for the tipoff. Those few extra moments spent at the concession stand were long enough for him to just miss the players coming out onto the floor.

As Marcus settles in his seat he anxiously looks over at the home team's bench to see if he can spot Darnell. There is no sign of him. With each pass that his eyes make along the team's bench Marcus looks more and more disappointed. But then, just like that, Darnell comes running out onto the sideline. He is late to the party because he slipped and fell in the locker room right before they were supposed to come out. One of the trainers kept him to bandage up his wrist. Of course, Darnell is focused on the game and doesn't spot Marcus in the stands. Marcus notices Darnell though and lights up. He claps as loud as anyone possibly can at the sight of the young man.

Even though his wrist is bandaged, he is still dressed to play. As the game gets underway, the battle is hard fought from the start. You can tell it's an important game because the tension is high and the game starts with a bunch of fouls being called. The first half is a back and forth battle with neither team having any more than a six point advantage. At the start of the second half the home team is down by eight points and is in serious foul trouble. Darnell has yet to enter the game and continues to cheer and support more than anyone on the team or in the stands. That's just the way he is. He has only played a few minutes this year and doesn't expect to play this game either. But with only two minutes left in a tie game, a fight breaks out on the court. A UCLA guard was driving hard to the basket. And as he was in the air, a member of the opposing team nailed him with a hard elbow to the jaw.

It is hard to tell whether it was done on purpose or not but either way it was enough to make the player miss the shot and fall to the floor in obvious pain. The home team doesn't take too kindly to that and they all rushed onto the court to support the rest of their team that is now in a fight under the basket. When the other team does the same all hell breaks loose. After twenty minutes, order is finally restored but only after a record six players were ejected from the game. With a minute left in regulation the Bruins are down by two and another player of theirs fouls out. With nobody else to call on, the coach looks over and says "Okay Darnell, get in there!" The stress and pressure that comes with this situation is something that is hard to compare. When he has not played all game or all season and has a freshly sprained wrist, his heart must be racing. Darnell looks very nervous and the coach sees it, so as the team heads back on the floor after a timeout, the coach grabs Darnell by the arm and says "Don't worry son. Just do your best!"

As the buzzer sounds the Bruins are ready to put the ball in play. Marcus is blown away at the magnitude of the moment and if anybody in the world can come close to the stress level of Darnell, it's Marcus. He can be seen in the stands with his hands together as if he is praying. Aside from the fight, it's been a terrific game and it's a shame a team has to lose. The Bruins are struggling to get the ball in play and with one second on the inbound clock a rocket of a pass is thrown into a Bruins player under the basket and the score is all tied up again. With 0:12 on the clock the other team has the ball and quickly hits a 10' foot jumper.

It's up to this last possession for the Bruins

and the fans in the jam packed Pavilion are on the edge of their seats. The Bruins quickly bring the ball up court and Darnell is trying desperately to work himself free to get the ball. With no other options the other guard spots an open Darnell and rifles the ball over to him. As if it was in slow motion, Darnell sees the ball coming towards him and can't believe that the outcome of this game and their whole season rest on his shoulders.

The moment is just too much for him and the second the perfectly delivered pass hits his hands it jars that freshly hurt wrist something awful and the ball goes through his hands and out of bounds at mid court. He puts his head down in disgust and the crowd puts out a collective sigh. The place becomes dead quiet With 3.0 seconds remaining and the other team bringing the ball in. A number of people begin to make their way to the exits.

The whole team gets deflated except for one. Darnell is on his man like glue but reads the eyes of the inbound passer and anticipates the pass. He breaks away from his man and stretches out at half court, off balance, to tip the ball away from the intended player. With his momentum, he is the one nearest the ball. But the ball is heading out of bounds. Remarkably, Darnell manages to grab the ball before it does go out of bounds but now he is headed out of bounds. He then makes the most incredible circus move of any player all year. He manages to twist his body enough in mid air to hurl a prayer of a shot just before the buzzer sounds. Darnell was just trying to get it close enough for someone to try and tip it in. As the ball is in the air the buzzer sounds and the ball banks hard off the backboard and into the basket.

The announcer screams hysterically "The Bruins win! The Bruins win!" and the crowd goes completely nuts. It's deafening. The entire team rushes over to Darnell who fell into the seats and lifts him onto their shoulders. It's a madhouse. All the players are jumping around. All the fans are jumping around. One announcer looks over to the other and says "You have got to be kidding me. That has to be the greatest hustle play of all-time."

It's a grand moment for everyone, especially the young man who suddenly has a bunch of microphones in his face. He has never had that before. It's always been everyone else. One of the reporters says "Tell us, what were you thinking as you threw the ball up?" Before he answers a teammate sticks his head in the camera frame and rubs Darnell's head. "That's why we call him the 'Hustler'," he says while continuing on his way to the locker rooms.

As Darnell begins to answer the question, he notices the man that saved him and his mother. Marcus made his way onto the court and was just standing there and clapping. Darnell can hardly believe his eyes. It's been a while since he had seen him and it was only that one time at the shelter. But when he locks eyes with him and sees Marcus give a fist pump when they look at each other, he knows.

Darnell says "I'm sorry, I have to go." to the reporter and he runs over to the waiting Marcus. They jump into each other's arms and act like they are father and son. His mother wasn't there even though she loves her son like crazy. She hasn't made a game all season because of her condition. She would have gotten too nervous and didn't want her son to be distracted. She watches the games on cable. It's the first time

Darnell has had someone come to see him play. And it's the man that he has thought of often. "Way to go Darnell," says Marcus. "What are you doing here?" asks Darnell. "I moved out here and I heard you were on the team so I came to see you play."

"I need to get into the locker room. Can you meet me near the entrance in an hour," asks Darnell. "Of course," replies Marcus. An hour later Darnell meets a waiting Marcus and they begin to walk and talk. Darnell tells Marcus that his apartment is close by and he wants him to come over. "My mother talks about you all the time. She will be blown away if you show up with me. Could you please come?" he asks. It's a cold night, even for California, so they talk while blowing into their hands to keep warm. "I would like nothing more," replies Marcus. Along the way people in the street recognize Darnell as the guy who hit the shot and people yell from their balconies or from passing cars. "Way to go Maclamore!" they say.

As they approach the apartment, Marcus goes on to tell Darnell how proud he is off him. "I knew there was something special about you the second I saw you. I never had any children but if I did have a son, I wish he would be just like you." Right before they enter, Darnell turns to Marcus and says "I never knew my dad because he left when I was a kid but if he was half the man you are, he would have been a great dad. Thank you for everything." Darnell says it with the most heartfelt look is his eyes that anyone could possibly have.

They agree to have Darnell go in first and have Marcus enter after he warns his mom that someone is here. The minute he opens the door his mom is at the entrance in her wheelchair with her arms stretched outwards. "I watched the game honey. You were great! I'm so very proud of you. You must have been so nervous," she says. "Thanks mom. I was very nervous," he replies as he bends down to give her a hug. "I have a surprise. Somebody came to watch me play and wanted to come by and say hello to you," Darnell says. "What are you talking about?" she asks while attempting to sit up a little straighter "Come on in," he says to a waiting Marcus.

The minute Marcus enters the room, Darnell's mother can't control herself and she begins to cry and cry. Marcus is not so sure why she is crying and thinks that perhaps there is something wrong so he walks over to her and puts his arm on her shoulder. The moment he does that, she takes that opportunity to throw her arms around his neck and draw him in even closer. In his ear she speaks in a broken up voice. "You are an angel. I pray for you every day. You gave us a chance to make it. You gave Darnell a chance at a happy life. From the bottom of my heart, thank you."

A very modest Marcus quietly replies back by saying "I'm nobody special. It just seemed like the right thing to do." At that point she wipes away the tears and rolls herself into the kitchen to get them something to drink. Darnell has always been there like a good son but has also always walked the fine line between being helpful and doing too much. She always told him since he was a little kid "I still want to be able to do things myself. Plus, you also need to live your own life."

After about an hour of talking, Marcus excuses himself because it's getting late and he doesn't want to wear out his welcome. He writes his cell phone number down on a pad of paper near the phone and says to his mom "If there is something you need just let me know." And with that, he hugs her again and leaves. Darnell decides to go have a coffee with Marcus and talk a little longer before he meets up with some teammates that are hanging out in Westwood Village and celebrating their big victory. After they sit for a while having a coffee, Darnell fills Marcus in on all the things happening in college and his life. Marcus returns the favor and shares with him what is going on in his life. He tells him he quit his job because he wasn't happy anymore and what made him decide to move to the west coast.

Marcus makes sure just to play up the angle of wanting a change and doesn't mention that Darnell was the one of the main reasons for his moving there. He also doesn't mention anything to Darnell about the wealth he once had and that now he has very little to show for all those years of hard work. However, he does mention that he is having a tough time finding work and encourages the young man not to give up on school and to take it as far as he can. He says it even though he knows he really doesn't need to.

It was a great visit with Darnell but Marcus

says "Good night" to his young friend with the promise of talking again soon and heads back to his car. After an action filled day it's time to go back home and get some rest. He isn't twenty one anymore.

Back at the apartment, Marcus falls into his chair in front of the television and only then really feels how worn down he is. He has never fully healed from the attack. He does gather a little more energy when he thinks back to the chance encounter with that beautiful woman earlier in the evening. Finally, a woman he seemed to have made a connection with. He reaches in his shirt pocket to discover the card is no longer there. Frantically, he checks all his pockets to only come up empty.

Although he has become accustomed to things not working out so well with love interests, this one hurts a bit more than the rest. He felt like it had a lot of promise. With all the jumping around at the game it must have fallen out and went unnoticed. "Oh well," he says aloud. He turns on some music and lays on his bed reflecting on life. There is a full moon tonight and the wind blows ever so slight. The first thing that

Marcus reflects on is where he stands financially and he doesn't focus on what he had from a materialistic point of view.

Over time, Marcus has gone from trying to realize his wants to focusing on his true needs. It started when his wife left. He knows that all women are not the same but he also feels time has run out. His days of having kids of his own are seemingly over because he feels strongly that he needs to be of certain age. Not only to properly care for his children, but he doesn't want to cheat the kids out of having a father figure that can physically take part in interacting with them. He wants to be able to relate on some level. It's the only regret he has ever had in his life.

As Marcus's eyes shut he begins to dream. There he is once again; eight years old and having his mom bend down in front of him to be at the same level. "It's alright honey, life is great, and we have each other. As long as we have that, we have everything we need," she says. He smiles and hugs her. To his dad, who sits and reads the paper, "Dad, do you want to play catch or something?" Marcus asks. His dad lowers the paper, and with a smile that can light up a room, responds by saying

"Are you kidding, let's go." Then finally, the scene that troubles him the most. It's the two of them waving goodbye as they leave him at the neighbor's house. He has had this exact dream thousands of times. It used to scare him but now he takes comfort in it.

Two weeks later Marcus can once again be found in a coffee house. But this time it's in Los Angeles instead of New York. He looks in the paper's classified section. It's nervous time. Marcus sees so few positions available. He resorts to looking at job positions in fields that he has no experience in. Marcus just can't bring himself to look for something that he had been doing most of his working career. He wants a new direction for his life. He is so tired of making money for those who really don't need it or losing money for those who can't afford to lose it. No matter how desperate he becomes he is destined to make a change.

Over the course of the next 2 months Marcus goes to a number of interviews for positions that ranged from a school janitor to a security guard. His generosity has cost him dearly. He has gone from over a million dollars in the bank to twelve hundred and no cents. Look at him in the street or talk to him face to face and you would never know it. That huge smile that he constantly wears is not for show. It's real. He always thinks that there are others out there worse off than him and he has no right to complain.

Even though his self perceived needs have gotten much smaller in scale, he is not without a survival instinct. That is one of the many reasons he left New York. He did not want to be subjected to the comments that would have certainly come his way. This way he can personally struggle more while those he helped can struggle a little less. Either way, the sun will shine on his face in Los Angeles. He was tired of the cold anyway.

Each one of the jobs he applied for was quickly filled by someone else more qualified and already experienced in that field. He really didn't stand a chance but he tried anyway because he knows enough to realize that nothing is going to come to him. He has to go get it. For the first time he shows some frustration and wrinkles up this morning's classified section of the paper and throws it across the room. "This is ridiculous!" he shouts out. With all the time he has spent on his laptop and getting the paper, he is no closer today to getting a job than when he first started looking some time ago. He is so sick of reading how the government keeps claiming that jobs are being created and things are getting better. He sees absolutely no evidence of it.

This day he decides to get in his car and take a drive. He just wants the sun to shine on his face as he drives around listening to the radio. Marcus really hasn't explored much of the Los Angeles area and figures this is a good opportunity to drive downtown and check out what is happening there.

As if he were in a movie, the images of empty store fronts, foreclosed homes and homeless people seem to be all that he can notice. He doesn't pay much attention to the type of architecture there is or the number of trees that line a given street. Instead, he looks at the faces of the homeless. He is taken back a bit by the number of people living on the street. That is because he didn't take the freeway and took side streets all the way. And now, he is near the Skid Row area.

It's clear, even to him, that he is in no position to help these people. There are just way too many of them. So, he drives on. It used to be that he thought there were enough jobs to be had and, other than with the exception of being sick, not getting some kind of a job was more a reflection of not putting forth the appropriate effort or having enough of a desire. He doesn't feel that way anymore. He looks at all those who are barely hanging onto jobs because of downsizing and all the people who are trying hard to find any kind of job that now he knows that there just aren't enough jobs out there. Not everyone can be an entrepreneur.

If he had the money, he would go down to Skid Row and places similar and take over a number of buildings all close to each other and create small factories. He would figure out some goods to produce that could and would be consumed by those in the area and elsewhere. He would want to keep the money flowing in the local community. Then he would take some of the buildings and convert them to free housing for those working in those factories. They would also get minimum wage for life's other essentials. For the resident workers, there would be a school for children of any age to become educated and 3 meals a day are provided free of charge.

It's Marcus's nature to think and dream. He continues to listen to music and come up with more ideas as he heads back home. He thinks about how he would have these units no bigger than a studio apartment complete with kitchenette and bathroom. They would be small places but their own places. It would be a place to save lives and build confidence. Under the age of 18 you can stay with your parent or parents at this place as long as you go to school there. Over 18 and you would be required to work there in order to stay.

Not having the burden of paying for rent will allow most of the workers to save or invest in themselves and turn into those entrepreneurs or at least create the desire to move on to better things and bigger places. If their performance is not up to the desired level after training or they are unable to work, they can't stay there. People would also be required to invest a certain number of hours to helping that community. It could be helping at the daycare that is provided or maintaining the place, but they would have to do something for others a little each month. They could even volunteer to help out with the communal garden that helps feed everyone. They might even try working in the kitchen

The surrounding area would be wiped clean and those not wanting that kind of assistance would be forced to move from there. There wouldn't just be factory jobs on the inside; there would be full time grounds keepers and security. There would even be a couple guys that are responsible for the removal of any graffiti. It would be the fastest graffiti removal system out there. Every morning those guys would comb the building's exteriors and mere moments after discovering graffiti the worker reaches behind him, in the golf cart, and begins to paint right over it. They would even have tons of the same color paint, that the building was painted, in order to show no evidence of it. It will frustrate the hell out of the taggers and they will eventually move on.

It won't be a perfect program, as few are. But it's a start. It's something. Those longing to be saved can look at it like a second chance while

94

those wanting nothing to do with it can figure something else out on their own. It's got to be better than watching whole families forced onto the street. Marcus finally returns home and turns off the music as he parks his car in his designated space. After entering his apartment he makes himself a cup of coffee and sits down at the table to write out the ideas he just had. He looks out the window as he reflects back on what he noticed during the drive. And then, it suddenly dawns on him.

He rarely ever drove in New York and he did what most everyone does and used mass transit. It felt good to him to sit in the car and soak in the sun. "That's what I'll do," he exclaims aloud. The plan is to do what it is that the other guy is doing. He is going to do what it takes to become an independent taxi driver using his own car. At this stage of his life he is not hung up on images and false pride. Whatever money he can earn is more than what is coming in now so he figures he has nothing to lose. A month later, Mr. Proactive has everything in order. After some adjustments are made to his car, he is ready for business.

As soon as he was ready to get the business going, Marcus went back to the hotel that he had stayed at for a while and met with the manager whom he became friendly with. "Hey Frank, I just started this taxi business. Would you leave some of these business cards on your counter here for your customers?" he asked. "I'm driving them myself," he added. "For you, no problem my man," replies Frank. Frank likes Marcus because of his demeanor. When Marcus left the lobby of the hotel that day, the manager didn't do what so many would have and toss them in the trash. He actually said to the staff behind the counter "I want you guys to use him."

The phone rings with his first call. It's at 9:05 p.m. on the 3rd of February, 2011. He marks the date and time on his pocket calendar that he keeps with him all the time. It's a woman asking to be picked up at the very hotel he left the cards at. "I'll be there in 20 minutes," he says to her. With that, Sunlight Taxi Company is launched.

He can't believe his eyes. When he exits the car to go get the customer in the lobby he notices the woman he met at the basketball game. The woman whose number he lost. "What a break," he mumbles to himself. At first she thinks that they are just bumping into each other again and she's kind of excited. Marcus tells the woman that he is actually there to pick her up. And when he does, her body language and tone change. She is confused because she had assumed he was successful based off of the way he was dressed at the game and even now.

Marcus notices the change in her right away and doesn't bother trying to explain to her that he had been very successful and had a lot of money at one point. He doesn't want to be judged on what he has or what he doesn't have. He wants to be judged on who he is. So, he doesn't even try to engage her in conversation. It's all business. "Where to?" he asks. You can see in his eyes that he is a little hurt. But he is used to it and will move on.

After a full week of business Marcus had ten phones call from customers wanting to be taken somewhere. Although he is not unhappy with his first week's performance, he is not satisfied either after doing some calculations on a piece of paper. As he sips on a cup of coffee at his table near the kitchen window, he decides that he needs to get out on the street and drive around searching for business instead of waiting for it to come to him. So the next day, that is what he does. He gets in the car and drives around for a while.

Forever planning and thinking, Marcus has a legal pad of paper on the passenger seat with a big title reading "What I would do if I could" It's there for whenever ideas come to him. He can write them down. This pad is strictly dealing with developing that area he drove through the other day. He heads back in that direction to get more ideas. He knows it won't be a good place to pick up paying customers but he figures that maybe along the way he can get something going. It's not his style to sit in a long line of other taxi drivers at the airport or similar places. He would rather go it alone.

Feeling a bit hungry, Marcus pulls into the parking lot of a hamburger place he has never seen before. On his way out of the restaurant he is approached by a young white man. He can't be anymore than sixteen or seventeen. The boy nervously approaches Marcus. Marcus doesn't feel threatened in any way because the boy isn't approaching him in a thuggish way. It looks like he has been roughed up and sleeping outside. "I'm sorry to bother you sir. Can you spare some money?" he asks. Normally, Marcus would have reached into his pocket and gave him some but for the first time in his adult life he responds "I'm sorry son, I don't have any."

He had to give almost everything he had to pay this month's rent. And it was late on top of that. That's why he feels the need to go out and get some business. He took the last $8.00 in his pocket to buy the hamburger and fries. Usually, he doesn't eat that kind of food but he's just in that kind of mood. Marcus looks into the boy's eyes and sees that they begin to water. He also looks down to see that the boy isn't wearing any shoes. "Thank you anyway," says the boy as he turns and begins to walk away. "Wait!" Marcus replies. "Are you hungry?" Marcus asks the boy. "I just want to go home," the boy says in a cracking voice as he begins to cry.

Marcus asks what his name is and he says "Jordy." When asked, Jordy goes on to explain how he had run away from his home in Nevada six months ago. He felt that he was treated unfairly by his parents for doing poorly in school. He knows now that it really wasn't true because they did little more than express concern, offer to help and keep on him about his study habits. It's only now that he wished he had put a little more effort into it and he is now ready to do that. "I just wish things were like before," he tells Marcus. Jordy had called his frantic parents a couple of weeks after he left to let him know that he was alive but when his dad raised his voice out of pure worry, Jordy hung up and hasn't called back since. Even though he has wanted to several times, he got robbed at gunpoint just two days after that and never did. They took the few things he had.

Since then, he has lived off of whatever he can beg for. Marcus hands him the bag of food and says "You can eat it in my car," while he opens the back door for him. The young man must be very hungry because he makes quick work of it and says "Thank you very much sir." At that moment, Marcus says "Let's go!" Jordy looks at him with a puzzled look on his face. "Go where?" he asks. "Let's get you home," replies Marcus as he looks at Jordy through the rearview mirror.

"You are going to drive me all the way there?" asks Jordy. "You got it. And you can call me Marcus," says Marcus. The boy has never heard news so good. He can't contain himself and acts like the boy he really is inside. He pumps his fist in the air multiple times while shouting "Yes, Yes, Yes."

Realizing that he has no cash on him and now has only $240.00 in the bank, he is going to have to live on credit for a while until things get rolling. It was the setting up of the business that put him over the edge but he figured he had to spend it to make it. At least he has plenty of room on his credit card. He doesn't want to just stick the kid on a plane or a bus and hope he makes it. He is going to make sure he makes it.

Jordy tells him the address and Marcus enters it into his newly bought GPS unit. After an hour of driving, Jordy falls asleep in the back seat. As the sun goes down it begins to get cold and Marcus tries to turn on the heater but for some reason it doesn't work. "You got to be kidding me," he mumbles aloud. Seeing that the boy is beginning to huddle up in a ball, Marcus gets off the freeway at the nearest exit while they are still in a populated area. He turns off the car and wakes Jordy. "Wait here, I'll be back in a few minutes. What size shoe do you wear?" he asks.

Half asleep, Jordy says "A size 10." Marcus says "That's funny, me too." as he shuts the door and heads towards the store. Finding a pair of tennis shoes on sale Marcus makes his way to the counter to pay for it. He can't believe his ears when the clerk says "I'm sorry sir, this card didn't go through. Do you have another one you want to try?" Marcus is completely caught off guard. He is shocked. He has that one credit card and his debit card.

He never used credit that much because he believes in not being in debt if at all possible. But survival is another story. Even though this card has had a balance of $6,000.00 for the last few months, it has a $15,000.00 limit on it. It should be working fine. He shakes his head and leaves the store empty handed. He wasn't about to take the last few dollars out of his checking account. He knows he will need that for gas and to get something for them to eat. It's going to be on the cheap but they would have to eat. Now that he can't afford to get a room to spend the night in, after the long drive there, it looks like he is going to have to spend the evening sleeping in the car.

Returning to the car, he notices Jordy is up and patiently waiting in the back seat. Amazingly, this is the very first time in a couple of years that Marcus isn't dressed up. He is in jeans, tennis shoes and a casual shirt with a casual jacket. Getting back in the car he looks at Jordy and says "Here, put these on," as he takes off his shoes and jacket. It's really cold and the boy, without hesitation, complies. At this moment Marcus remembers he had gone to the mailbox before he left his apartment and collected his mail. He had planned to open it while waiting at traffic lights or stopped somewhere but forgot about it in the glove box. He remembered seeing his credit card bill and something else from the credit card company.

He didn't think anything of it because he is well below his limit and he is never late with a payment. He had hardly used it up until recently, but a lot of purchases have gone on there and he has been riding that debt for a longer than normal time frame with only the minimum payments being made.

As he opens it and reads the first paragraph of the letter he finds out that it is exactly because of those reasons that the company had just up and cut his limit to $500.00 over where his balance was at the time. Not knowing that, he had made a purchase of $550.00 just a couple days later. When looking at his bill he discovers that he is now over his new limit and was charged an over the limit fee. Now, he can't even use that card at all. These are unchartered waters he has wondered into.

He can do nothing other than forge ahead. They are only a couple of hours away now and the boy begins to recognize some of the surrounding area because of local trips his family had made. You can see him sit straighter and become more energetic. After the toughest six months of this young man's life, he is ready to work hard and be part of his family's everyday life once again. "I hope they will love me again," he tells Marcus. A cold Marcus looks in the rearview mirror and says "They never stopped."

After filling up the car with gas once

again, they are minutes away. Then it finally happens, they turn down his street and Jordy says "It's that one," as he points to the big house on the corner. At 5:30 a.m. on a Tuesday morning Jordy is finally home. Marcus sits in the car across the street to watch the exchange from a distance.

The door opens and his father yells "Jordy is home!" at the top of his lungs. Both Jordy and his father put their arms around each other in what can only be described as the most heartfelt and loving hug in the history of hugs. His dad lifts the young man off his feet. Then his mother and sister come running out of their rooms and join in a massive family hug.

It's at that point that Marcus knows the young man will be fine and he turns the car around and leaves. He didn't stay long enough to be noticed by the family when Jordy turned around to point in his direction.

Marcus is dead tired now and looks for somewhere to park and sleep for a couple of hours before driving home. He finds a side street not too far from the boy's home. It's a quiet residential neighborhood so he takes a chance and pulls over under a tree. He is cold and is having the worst 3 hour nap he has ever had. The last thing in the world he wants to do is now drive from Nevada to Southern California. But with little to no choice, he presses on. He is very worried about having enough money to get home. He had not planned on his credit card being frozen and driving to Nevada and back.

"Please God, let me make it home," he says aloud as he stares into the blue sky. He wants little more right now than to be at his apartment in his bed. His love of music keeps his spirits up as he listens to different types on the radio and begins the very long drive home. Halfway home he pulls over once again to get gas. He is absolutely starving but is very worried about not making it all the way. Parking the car at pump #8 he does some calculating on the back of his legal pad in the passenger seat. He is figuring how much gas he has already used, how far he has gotten from point A to point B and looking to see what his balance would be now after spending what he has. He isn't using the numbers provided by the car dealer.

After he finishes, he concludes that if he

only spent the remaining balance of cash in his bank on gas he may just make it. There wasn't a dollar to spare on anything to eat. But then he remembers how one day he had tossed some change in the glove box. He opens it up and digs through it. You would think he just won the lottery when he is able to scrape up $2.36 in coins from amongst the lose papers.

Normally this very proud man cares about how he looks and presents himself but with no shoes, messed up hair, wrinkled clothes and being cold, he puts gas in the car with little concern for how he looks. When finished, he puts the nozzle back in the holder and walks towards the entrance of the minimart. Just feet from the door he steps in a puddle and gets he sock all wet on his right foot. "That's great!" he says in a slightly frustrated tone.

The man behind the counter has been having trouble with homeless people loitering around his establishment and is quick to spot Marcus entering. "Get out of here you bum!" says the old man. It's not totally his fault because with the way Marcus looks at the moment most people would think the same thing.

Marcus looks at him and pulls out his wallet. "Sir, that is my car out there and I just put gas in it." Then he opens his hand to reveal the change and says "I just want to buy a couple of hot dogs and I'm leaving." The man agrees and hands him his two cents in change. He sits in the car and inhales both hot dogs in record time. He still has some water remaining in the car. Marcus hasn't eaten this poorly in a very long time but that is the last thing on his mind. Something is better than nothing.

This seemingly never ending journey is about to end. At long last, Marcus spots his exit off the freeway. At the same time, he looks down at the gas gauge and it's below empty. For the last few miles he has been running on fumes. He's got it. He is only two blocks away when after a series of lunges and jolts the car comes to a halt. He manages to steer towards the curb. "Man, so close!" he says to himself. He is right in front of someone's driveway; otherwise he would just leave it and deal with it in the morning. So, he has to try and move a few car lengths to get out of the way. He may end up getting it towed and that is the last thing he wants. So, in his socks, he gets out and pushes. It's hard on his feet and he struggles but he manages to get it rolling.

With the slight momentum that he has, he is going to try to make it all the way. Suddenly a car that was driving by pulls over and stops. Instead of being some man, who you may expect, it's a woman that gets out of the car. Not only is it a woman, but she is Latina, in her mid forties, and dressed in a pantsuit and high heels. He stops to look at this beauty walk towards him. "Can I help?" she asks.

Stuck for words he has a hard time spitting out "That would be great." He can't believe this professional woman in her expensive sedan stopped and offered to help. She gets into the driver seat to steer and that way he can put all his muscle into it. She sticks her head out of the rolled down window and says "Where are we going?" Marcus points down the street and replies "You see that moving van down there. I'm right next to it." This ever so pleasant woman with the sweetest smile says "No way! That is me moving in." Marcus simply can't believe his ears and his good fortune. Even if she is married, it's going to be cool just to look at her from time to time.

Three young men come running down the street to help. "Those are my sons coming. They are helping me move in. You can stop, they will do it," she says. He appreciates the help and listens to her. He has pushed himself well past the maximum limit his body has set. Each young man has her same smile and they all say "Hello" before grabbing hold and pushing. With all of them, the car is really moving now and he can't keep up. Marcus trails the group but walks as fast as he can.

A couple minutes later, when Marcus catches up, formal introductions are made. Tired, dirty and hungry he just wants to get inside. Since Marcus was a little boy he has had a tendency to squirrel things away for a rainy day. Sometimes he forgets that he has already gotten it or may just forget where he hid something but he vaguely remembers squirreling a few dollars away. Not because he envisioned all this happening but he knows that you never can tell what might happen. It came from being a boy at that group home.

Before he does anything else, he goes straight to the back of his closet in his bedroom behind a pile of sweaters and finds it. It's $500.00

cash. Little did he know at the time how important that was. That one act will allow him to get enough gas for the week and some food. It will allow him to be able to try to earn some money throughout the week. He is going to take tomorrow off though.

The next morning, the beautiful Ms. Sanchez is about to get into her car and head to work as an advisor in the Mayor's office. A cup of coffee in one hand and a briefcase in the other, she notices a yellow pad of paper in the street. Because of her inquisitive nature and her just liking things to be clean, she retrieves it. Since she is in a rush she takes it with her into her car with the intention of seeing if she can figure out whom it belongs to.

As she stops at traffic signals her eyes continue to be drawn toward the title of the writings on the pad that sits on her passenger seat. She repeats it out loud. "What I would do if I could." She doesn't look at the details written or even the summary because she is concentrating on her big meeting and she is running a little late. But all day long those words bounce around in her head. It just sticks with her. She looks forward to going home and having a cup of tea and investigating a little.

Normally Marcus is an early riser but this morning sleeping in is the general theme he is working with. When he finally does get up and makes himself a cup of only the finest in plain wrap coffee, he notices that his pad is missing. Life won't end if he doesn't find it but with the time he has invested in it already he would sure like to come across it and not have to do it all over again and possibly forget things.

He looks around the apartment and can't find it. He goes outside and looks up and down the street and can't find it. Then finally, he just gives up. While outside, he receives a call. The light flashes on his message machine letting him know when he enters. When he presses the button a man speaks.

"Marcus, my name is Justin. I'm Jordy's father. I want to thank you so much for bringing Jordy home to us. The entire family wants to thank you. I'm certain you saved his life. Actually, you saved us all. The family has been a wreck since he left and now we can finally be whole again. Please call me back as soon as you can. I would like to talk to you." Marcus picks up the phone right away.

A jubilant Justin picks up the phone knowing that it is Marcus. He has caller identification. Marcus can barely get out "Hi, this is Marcus." before Jordy's dad has thanked him another 8 times. He goes on to explain that he is a columnist for the Newspaper there. "I was hoping you would allow me to do a story on what you did," he says. "That isn't necessary," replies Marcus. Justin pleads with him and says that it would make him and his family happy because it's the only way they knew how to really thank him. A reluctant Marcus agrees but says "I'm sure anybody else would have done the same." Justin is quick to disagree and says "That is where you are wrong. Most people would not have. You have a kind soul."

7 days pass and Marcus hasn't received one call for his taxi service. He is becoming quite concerned. Meanwhile, Ms. Sanchez is in her apartment after a long day of work and she is shocked to see a picture of the man she helped,

the man living in her building. She is quick to grab the remote control and turn up the volume. At the same time, Darnell happens to be at his apartment with his mother and he sees the same picture on the same channel and says to his mother "Mom, they are talking about Marcus, come here." She rolls over and they both watch.

Apparently, the newspaper article struck a chord with readers and it quickly got picked up by the local television station that ran with it. Darnell, his mother, and Ms.Sanchez are all overwhelmed with emotion. An animated Darnell bounces around the room, just happy to know the man. "You go Marcus. Marcus, you are the man!" he keeps saying. He picks up the phone and calls the television station and tells them all about what that same person did for him and for the shelter in New York. Ms. Sanchez just fell in love.

Marcus never sees the article or the segment on television. But, he knows something is different because all of a sudden the phone is ringing off the hook for people wanting a ride from Sunlight Taxi Service. The tips he is beginning to receive are larger than anticipated. Over the course of the next few days Ms. Sanchez makes a few attempts to talk to Marcus by knocking on his door. But they keep missing each other because of their conflicting schedules. She finally leaves a note on his door inviting him over to her apartment for a cup of tea.

All along, Ms. Sanchez keeps looking for clues as to who wrote these detailed notes laying out a plan of growth for an area that is in desperate need of it. She doesn't want to put it back in the street and the ideas contained on those lined sheets make sense and seem viable. She believes in those words and ideas so much that she has been trying to form them into an official presentation that would be submitted to the Mayor and those in city government. All along she has told everyone that she came across the information and she isn't the author or creator. She is an honest woman.

At 6:05 p.m. on a Friday evening, Marcus pulls into his parking space after a long day of driving people around and notices the beautiful Ms. Sanchez's car parked next to him. He takes this opportunity to come calling. He fixes himself up a little before he knocks. When he does, the blinds in her kitchen get pulled back just a little for her to see who it is. She looks grubby from cleaning the kitchen and is even wearing yellow rubber gloves. She quickly yanks her gloves off and throws them in the corner and pulls the bandana off her hair that was holding it back. She wastes no time in opening the door.

She seems a little nervous all of a sudden but still invites him in for a cup of tea despite not being at her most glamorous. Little does she know that Marcus loves what he is seeing and how he's feeling. Before he is able to sit down at the table Ms. Sanchez grabs him unexpectedly and gives him a hug and a kiss on the cheek. "What was that for?" he asks. "For saving that boy," she replies.

Just then, he notices his legal pad on her kitchen counter and says "Oh, great! You found my pad." As soon as he says that Ms. Sanchez becomes distracted and pours the hot water onto the counter instead of into the cups. "That's yours?" she asks. "Yes. I had been looking for that. Thanks for finding it." At that moment, the television in her kitchen shows Marcus's picture again. She reaches over to turn up the volume while saying "Hey look, they have something else about you." Marcus is embarrassed and begins to speak just as the news anchor is about to. However, Ms. Sanchez is quick to say "Honey, I want to hear what they are saying." That "Honey" she just threw out there got him to be quiet instantly. It puts a big smile on his face.

The news anchor says "Okay, we have more on the man that many are affectionately calling the Soul Driver." He goes on to give a detailed account of the things Marcus had done to help others. Ms. Sanchez says "We need to talk." 1 Year later the sun shines bright on the large crowd that has gathered in the Skid Row area." They are all there to celebrate the ground breaking of Project Sunlight. The clicking of the cameras can be heard all around as pictures are being taken of Marcus shaking hands with the Mayor and then doing the honors of shoveling the first scoop of dirt.

THE END

Made in the USA
Coppell, TX
03 January 2021